Mystic Saints Of India:6

Swami Vivekananda

B. K. CHATURVEDI

Series Editor : (Dr.) Mahendra

BOOKS FOR ALL

Delhi-110052

Distributed by
D. K. Publishers Distributors Pvt. Ltd.
24, Ansari Road, Darya Ganj
New Delhi-110 002
Phs. : 327 8584, 327 9215, 327 8368
Fax : 326 4368
E-mail : dkpd@del3.vsnl.net.in
Web site:www.dkpd.com.

First Published : 2002

ISBN 81-7386-244-3 (Swami Vivekanand)
ISBN 81-7386-231-1 (Series)

Published by
Books For All
(an imprint of Low Price Publications)
A-6, Nimri Commercial Centre,
Near Ashok Vihar Phase-IV, Delhi-110 052
Ph. : 740 1672, 745 2453
E-mail : lpp@nde.vsnl.net.in
Web site:www.lppindia.com.

Printed at
D. K. Fine Art Press Pvt. Ltd.
Delhi-110052 Ph. 745 2451

Printed in India

Introduction

This sixth flower of our bouquet is devoted to Swami Vivekananda, a unique spiritual leader of India, who introduced various unique Indian concepts to the west. His universal vision, rational approach and commitment to ameliorating the distressed humanity are still unparalleled in history of the fact that nearly a century has elapsed since he quit his mortal coil. Even then in his exhortations seem very relevant, particularly to the existing Indian conditions. That is why we have appended his chosen exhortations at the end to help our discerning reader feel the warmth that his words had inspired the world with. A brief life history of this great karma yogi give an idea as to how an ordinary Bengali boy, Naren, was transformed into 'Swami Vivekananda' once he met his mentor and Master, Swami Ramakrishna Paramahansa.

The events recorded here are authentic and devoid of any attempt to deify either him or his guru. The whole attempt has been to show how an honest quest turns a confused youth into a universal saint.

Lastly, the author conveys his gratitude to Mittal Brothers of 'Books For All' for giving him an opportunity to convey his regard through this slender volume to this great saint of India.

B.K. Chaturvedi

SERIES' EDITOR'S NOTE

In 1963, Dr. Radhakrishnan, the President of India, declared in Bombay, " The time has come for all countries to work towards making the world a single home for Humanity.....Economics, Politics and transport have done their jobs. But we have to do as to give a soul to the world which has found a body, you can give it if you are truly Indian." We Indians are proud to have so many mystic saints in our history who can contribute to the upliftment of humanity.

In the Indian philosophy, there are two modes through which we acquire knowledge: Argument and Experiment. Both these modes, together with experience play an important role in the development of mankind. Saints of India, through their arguments, tried to communicate their experiences which they represent an adventure in thinking.

This series, it is hoped, will enable the reader, eastern or western, to understand and appreciate currents of Indian thought depicting the life and writings of different saints. We have tried to portray the true picture of Indian culture.

I am really thankful to all those, who have helped in preparing and publishing these books, as they will not only propagate the ideas of Indian saints, but also help in making the mankind a better race. Our world, becomes wider, our imagination and life more colourful and enriched as a result of our companionship with these saints, who are the travellers of the spirit and the pioneers of thought.

25.7.01 **(DR.) MAHENDRA**

Contents

1

Swami Vivekananda: A Saint with Universal Vision

Swami Vivekananda was, perhaps, India's first spiritual emissary who enlightened the west about : the glory that India was? A great scholar; a man of dynamic energy and inspiring personality, he preached the supremacy of Vedantism. He was in fact a bridge between India's glorious past and its present. He was the first Hindu whose personality won demonstrative recognition abroad for India's civilisation.

He is, in many respect, quite comparable to Adi Shankaracharya. While the Adi gurus consolidated the faith in Aryavarta as India was known them, Vivekananda spread the seeds of Indian thought to the world at large. While the former formed a sect with the objective of keeping the ancient faith ever revived with dynamic approach, Vivekananda created a mission in the name of his master to take India's message to foreign shores. Both died young and both achieved in their short life span what lesser mortals would have taken centuries to accomplish.

Vivekananda was the only saint of that era who had universal vision. Whatever he said and did was meant to improve the lot of humanity. Though he did not believe in establishing a new creed, as for example Dayananda did, he wished to propagate the ancient religion of India where it was not so well-known and above all to serve humanity, to bring comfort to those tormented, and faith to those that were groping in the darkness of doubt. To his disciples his message was;

"Let's throw away all pride and learning and study of the *Shastras* (scriptures) and all *sadhanas* [disciplining of the mind by meditation etc.] for the attainment of *mukti* [emancipation] —and going from village to village devote our lives to the service of the poor, and by convincing the rich men about their duties to masses, through the force of our Character and spirituality and our austere living, get money and the means wherewith to serve the poor and distressed! Alas! nobody in our country thinks for the low, the poor and the miserable? Those that are the backbone of the nation, whose labour produces food, those whose one day's strike from work raises a cry of general distress in the city—where is the man in our country who sympathises with them, who shares in their joys and sorrows!"

Although the question raised by this saint is still unanswered, even after nearly one century passing away, yet his thinking as the saint encompassing the old concept "Vasudheiva kutumbakam" is quite apparent. May be, this type of concern might have been shown by other great persons but Vivekananda was different from them in one very glaring aspect. He was a true Karmayogi who also performed whatever he preached. He was not only an academic philosopher; not indeed one who believed in mere renunciation. In the spirit of the Gita, he believed in the active participation in various works. He worked at a breakneck speed, like Shankaracharya, for the welfare of humanity and died even before he was forty, vindicating the famous saying "great men are like meteors; they consume themselves to light the earth". Indeed he did so but he is not dead or extinguished because through his lectures and exhortations he is still awakening mankind.

Perhaps he was also the first Indian spiritual leader who could converse in the language understood by the west. When he spoke he didn't need any interpreters. His command over the English language also went a long way to make him have direct, heart to heart talks with his audience. Of course his influence did spread to non-English speaking countries as well but such countries also heard him with rapt attention because Vivekananda had acquired the idiom of the West. Although he didn't write any book as the thinkers of his time did, yet his exhortations convey genes not only from the content's but from the language's point of view also.

Yet another quality that distinguishes him from other scholars and thinkers of India is his laying especial emphasis on reason despite his talking about faith. There is an interesting episode related to his this quality which doesn't figure in the authentic literature about him but it reveals his pragmatic approach quite succinctly.

Once, it is said, that in interior Bengal he was waiting for a boat to cross a river. All of a sudden there came a Sadhu and contemptuously asked him: " Vivekananda ! It is claimed that you have shaken the whole West by your exhortation and that you are a great Karmayogi. But how come, despite all your learning you can't cross this tiny river walking afloat on water? See, how I do!" And that Sadhu started walking on water. By that time the boat had also arrived and Vivekananda also managed to reach the other bank of the river. The Sadhu was still there. Although he tried to behave insolently on account of his 'victory', Vivekananda was quite unruffled. He said to the Sadhu: "Maharaj! I admireYour Yogic powers. But may I ask as to what purpose you are employing the same in improving the lot of humanity and making the distressed happy. All that you have achieved by your exalted Yogic power is saving a couple of paisa that you may have to give to the boatman to cross the river by boat! Haven't you made worth of your power no good than a pittance. "The Sadhu was cut to his proper size. In fact this is what is the rare trait in this Swami's personality: he brought all to book beyond self. In one of his lectures he admitted that though India did have real Yogies, they didn't come forward to help all mankind and confirmed their prowess in showing miracles and earning a great name for themselves. Still we may be having the real ones but they fight shy in putting their powers to the benefit of entire humanity. For that matter, let alone entire humanity, they even lack the national outlook. Vivekananda was the first spiritual leader who gave a call to the nation. "Awake My India!" is his famous exhortation. His pragmatic approach saw it clearly that the salvation lay not only in coping with the west or sticking to the old beliefs with the advancement of the west and spiritual enlightenment of the east that was and is required to make man attain peace of mind and plenty of comforts for the body. As Shakespeare says:

For there was never a philosopher
That could endure toothache patiently.
[Much A Do About Nothing']

He was also against not only the ills of the east and the west but also about the wrongly interpreted beliefs. He believed that all can progress no matter how backward they are. Hence he was also against the so-called 'perfectionists.' He once said that a perfectionist was a person who waits for all water of the river to run down to the ocean before endeavouring to cross the river The sarcasm in this definition is too blatant to be missed. This is the attitude of a pragmatic person. Perhaps he acquired this trait from his mentor and master Swami Ramakriahna Paramahansa who also stressed on taking nothing for granted. Even he allowed his favourite disciple to test him before accepting him finally as the guru.

What makes Vivekananda eternally relevant is his exhorting the basic virtues in man. This is why he is as relevant to the modern world as Gandhi or Mother Teresa might be. For such thinkers defy all limitation of time and space since they try to awaken the real man.

2

Birth And Early Years

Swami Vivekananda or (as addressed) Narendranath Datta, or simply Naren as he was called in his pre-monastic days] was born in a renowned family of kshatriyas in Calcutta on January 12, 1863. His grand father, Durga Charan, was a strict follower of the traditional Hindu 'ashramas' (stages of life). After leading a family life, he quietly vanished and became a monk. All efforts to bring him back to family life were of no avail. In fact, Durgacharana had a spiritual bent of mind right from the beginning. But his son, Vishwanath Datta, who was Narendra's father, was a different person. Vishwanath was a man out of this world. For him religion was something to be taken recourse to on given occassions and hence was of no especial consequence to this famous attorney in the Calcutta High Court. Vishwanath had plenty of money and he wasn't a miser. He was also proficient in English and Persian, and took great delight in reciting to his family the poems of the renowned Persian poet Hafiz. He also enjoyed the study of the Bible and of the Hindu scriptures in Sanskrit. Though charitable to an extravagant degree and sympathetic towards the poor, Vishwanath was rationalistic and progressive in outlook in matters religious and social, owing perhaps to the influence of Western culture. His wife and Naren's mother Bhuvneshwari Devi, was an accomplished lady with a regal learning. She was deeply religious. Before Naren's birth, though she had daughters, she yearned for a son and asked one of her relatives at Varanasi (Kash) to make offerings to Vireshwara Shiv. It is said that she dreamt later that Lord Shiv promised to be born as her son. It was sometimes after this dream that Naren was born. Naren was the eldest male issue of the Datta family which had two more sons and four daughters.

Early childhood of Naren was marked with much fun and frolic. He was in fact, a restless child. However, right from childhood, he had a great attraction for spiritual matters and would play at worshipping or meditating on the images of Rama- Sita, Shiv etc. The stories of the *Ramayana* and the *Mahabharata* which his mother recited to him, left an indelible impression on his mind. Traits such as courage, sympathy for the poor, and attraction towards wandering monks appeared rather spontaneously in him. Even in his childhood, it was a habit with Naren to demand convincing arguments for every proposition. Although Naren loved his father and despite occasional outbursters he had great respect for his advice.

Nevertheless, Naren resembled his grandfather more than his father. He was charitable to monks particularly, and would never let any one of them go away empty handed. He had a strong, healthy body and a quick mind but his heart was full of tenderness. Love of truth, and a passion for purity distinguished him from ordinary boys. Being very fond of meditations, one day he got so lost in these meditations that his anxious relations had to force open the door of the room he was in and had to be forcibly shaken to bring back to consciousness. He used to have many visions, and mainly they divided themselves into two opposed categories. He would imagine himself to be a successful man of the world, as his father was, on a high post, commanding respect in society and plenty of money. Immediately after he would see himself as a wandering monk; wearing a loin cloth and begging for food from door to door. But he was more attracted to a life of renunciation rather than one of worldly fame and honour. Naren was also a proficient debater as his contemporaries would affirm.

Even when he was adolescent, Naren's leonine beauty was matched by his courage. He had the physique of an athlete, a resonant voice, and brilliant intellect. He distinguished himself in athletics, philosophy, and music and, among his colleagues was the undisputed leader. At college, he studied and absorbed western thoughts, and this implanted a spirit of critical inquiry in his mind. His inborn tendency towards spirituality and his respect for ancient religious traditions and beliefs on the one hand, and his argumentative nature, coupled with his sharp intellect, on the other, were now at war with each other. In this predicament, he tried to find comfort in the Brahmo Samaj, the popular socio-religious movement of the time. The Brahmo-Samaj believed in a formless God, deprecated the worship of idols and addressed itself to various forms of social reform. Though the Brahmo Samaj talked about Brahman, the impersonal aspect of God, they gave lectures, argued, debated and quoted scriptures, but none of them, not even the great Keshab Sen, had even a fleeting glimpse of God in any form, personal or impersonal. Even the great —Maharshi Devandernath started speaking in a round about manner when Naren asked that simple question: "Sir, have you seen God?

He found an answer to this question even in the Western philosophy which he studied during his college days with great diligence. Of course Mill, Descartes, Spinoza, Hume, Bentham, Darwin, Comte, Spencer and the renowned German philosophers like Kant, Hegel Schopenhauer did fascinate him and so did many ideas enunciated by them, but he found them too factual as they were based on pure reason. God seemed to have almost no place in them. So his simple question about God's existence remained unanswered.

Naren had had some extraordinary experiences right from childhood. Describing one of these later, he said that he would see a point of light between his eyesbrows, which would keep changing colours and growing in size till it became as big as a ball. Then it would spread all through his body and he would lose consciousness and fall asleep.

This way he would feel some inexplicable existence but all his efforts failed to make him learn anything about direct realisation of God. The question continued to haunt him even as he graduated from high school and started studying in the Presidency College of Calcutta. Naren joined the general Assembly's institution with history as his subject. He also studied European history and western logic and philosophy. Yet, inspite of imbibing western culture, Naren remained typically Indian in his outlook and habits. A strict vegetarian, he slept on the bare floor and never used more than one blanket. He also determined not to marry and get involved in family life, even though he had many tempting offers with one of the girls' father even agreeing to pay for his education in England which in those days was essential for entering the mighty Indian Civil Service.

All this while, his spiritual restlessness remained increasingly accentuated. He eventually got a way to get some peace when he once talked to Professor W.W. Hastie, a benevolent Englishman who was the principal of the General Assembly's institution. This Englishman, being kind-hearted didn't have the usual prejudice against the Hindu sages and he had met Ramakrishana once and was impressed by him. Hastie was also struck with Narendra's spiritual qualities. One day, speaking about such meditation in which one loses one's outer cousciousness, Hastie said that the only person whom he had known to achieve this was the Sage of Dakshineshwar, Ramakrishna. That was the first time Naren heard about his future master and mentor. However, having questioned Davendranath and other so-called Savants about God and recening only disappointment, Naren thought at first that was one more such ballyhoo, and didn't show much interest.

Their meeting eventually took place in November, 1881 when Surendranath Mitra celebrated the Durga Pooja. Naren was also called by him to sing devotional songs for the entertainment of the devotees gathered there. Naren happened to sing there with great fervour and feeling which charmed the entire audience including Ramakrishna, the special invitee for the function. The Sage of Dakshineshwar, as Ramakrishna was known at that time, was impressed by Naren. He studied the lad closely and found some divine spark. So he asked Naren to meet him at Dakshineshwar. But at that point of time Naren was busy with his studies. Another offer for his marriage also came around this time with a handsome dowry but it was also turned down.The intermediatory through whom this offer had come was one Ramchandra Datta. When he realised the verocity of Naren's deep spiritual longing which had come between the marriage and the political groom, he advised Naren that if he really wished to pursue this path he ought to go to Ramakrishna. He also told Naren that the Brahman couldn't ever satisfy him with his answers. Not only that, Ramchandra Dutta himself offerd to take him there.

This was the second time that Naren had been told that it was only Ramakrishna who could quench his spiritual thirst. He was impressed upon that key to his queries was only with the Sage of Dakshineshwar. He knew the way that led to God. So the resistance built in Narendra owing to his imbiding reasoning of the West and sceptism about the 'self-realised' souls was finally broken. The ground was prepared and the way was paved for 'reason' to seek refuge in 'faith'. Eventually, Narendra decided to go to Dakshineshwar. It was at this juncture that Narendra was also reminded of Prof. Hastie's words: " The Saint at Dakshineshwar had experienced the ecstasy described by Wordsworth in his poem " The Excursion". So with the question raking his mind Naren turned towards Daskhineshwar.

3

At The Feet of Sri Ramakrishna

Describing Naren's first visit to Dakshineshwar, the Sage, Ramakrishna, told his disciples much later,

Naren entered this room by the Western door. He seemed careless about his body and dress and unmindful of the outside world. His eyes indicated a mind which looks within, as though it was fixed on something. I couldn't imagine there could be such a spiritual man coming from Calcutta where everyone was seemingly running after material things. [He had brought some companions with him but they struck me to be just the ordinary kind who crave only for enjoyment]. There was a mat on the floor and I asked him to sit on it, and to sing some devotional songs. He sang with such fervour and devoutness, and there was so great pathos in his Bengali songs that I was moved and lapsed immediately into 'Samadhi'.

After the songs ended Ramakrishna came back into consciousness Then he suddenly arose and holding Naren by the hand, went to the veranda on the northern side. As the two some reached there the door was closed by the Sage. Naren was silent and bewildered. Then Ramakrishna, still holding Naren by the hand began to whisper while shedding tears profusely: "Ah! Why have you made so much of delay in coming to me? I have been waiting as if for ages for you. I am tired of listening to the talks of wordly people and my heart is bursting with the desire to reveal my inner most experience to someone who can really understand them." Still sobbing and standing there with folded hands, Ramakrishana said to Naren; "Lord! I am aware that you are Nara, the ancient sage, the incarnation of Narayana, born on the earth to remove mankind's misery. Thus Ramakrishna kept on speaking in the same emotion-charged strain for minutes. Naren was visibly taken aback. "Stark mad, this raving man, isn't he?' he thought. "Why must he say such things to me? How he could dare take so much of liberty from me. The rationalist in Naren kept on raising such irreverent questions. But outwardly he kept his peace. Then Ramakrishna went back to his room, and bringing some sweets began to feed Naren with his own hands. Naren was embarrassed. He said: "give them to me. I'll share them with my friends." But unmindfully, Ramakrishna kept on putting the sweets into Naren's mouth, while assuming: "You have this from me. Your friends will get afterwards. When the sweets' stock was finished, he caught Naren's hand lovingly and earnestly pleaded, "Promise that you will come to me again, soon, alone." When the Sage repeatedly invited Naren couldn't help saying: "I will try". Saying so a confussed Naren rushed back to the 'sane' company of his friends.

However, the moment they reached back the room there was no trace of such frenzic behaviour that the sage had shown before. This time he spoke coherently with a force of inner conviction. Then Naren thought of asking him about God as he had been doing so before all great and supposedly 'God realised' persons. On hearing the question the sage said with a firmness in his voice" "Yes! God can be seen and realised the same way as I am talking to you. It isn't a fake or concocted existence. But who cares to take pains to honestly pray to God or to listen to His voice. People shed torrents of tears for their wife and children but who sheds tears for the sake of God? If one weeps sincerely for him, he will surely manifest himself."

Ramakrishna's unambiguous assertion about God's existence and the possible access to Him with purity of feeling made Naren think and change his earlier opinion about the sage. 'Well, this man may be mad but, at the same time, he seems to be a true saint.' He speaks with inner conviction." Besides, in Ramakrishna's words Naren had found for the first time a positive answer to his repeated query about God. At last he had found someone who, for the first time, could say that god could be seen and realised. So be bowed before the sage in his renewed reverence and left.

Nevertheless, for an eighteen year old college student who had savoured the rationality advocated by the western philosophers, it was still a tough decision to believe which side lay the truth; whether the Sage of Dakeneshwar was a fake or a genuine god-realised soul. The mad ravings of the sage and his inner conviction filled sermons on the existence of God had put the lad in a fix. Once speaking to his western disciples the same Naren as Vivekananda had expressed: "Let no one think that the struggle to believe is an easy one. I know it is not, for I had resisted my Master continually for six long years."

So, if not out of anything but sheer curiosity he decided to keep his word to the sage and visited Dakshineshwar going all alone, all the way on foot. As he entered the Sage's room, he found him sitting alone. Seeing Naren, he joyfully muttered something and enthusiastically rose to welcome him. Naren was a little apprehensive lest they might have yet another crazy meeting full of ravings and 'rigamaroles' but as soon as this thought entered his mind, the Sage placed his hand over Naren's heart. Instantly Naren felt something he would never forget throughout his life. He felt as if everything before him was getting dissolved into naught—the walls, the floor, the roof and all the objects in that room. What existed there was a great void. Even Naren's own consciousness had vanished. To the bewildered lad it seemed as if he was facing death. So he cried in anguish: "What have you done to me? I have my parents at home!" At that moment Ramakrishna stroked Naren's chest and everything became as normal as before. Later on, Naren, as Vivekananda, was to describe this experience the following way: "All this happened in less time than it takes to narrate it. But it did revolutionise my mind. Amazed, I thought what it could possibly be. It came and went at the mere wish of this wonderful man. I began to question whether this was any kind of hypnotism! But that was not likely for these tricks affected only the weak minds, and I prided on being the anything but weak. I had not surrendered myself to the stronger personality of the man. Rather, I had taken him to be monomaniac. So what was this sudden transformation of mine due to? I couldn't come to any conclusion. It was an enigma which I thought I had better not attempt to solve. I was determined, however, to be on my guard and not to give any chance to exert a similar influence on men.

"The next moment I thought how could a man who metamorphosed at will, a strong mind like mine be dismissed as a lunatic? Yet this was the conclusion at which one would arrive from his effusions on the occasion of our first meeting, unless, of course he was an incarnation of God, which was indeed a far cry. So I was in a dilemma about the real nature of my experience as well as about this remarkable man, who was pure and simple as a child. My rationalistic mind received an unpleasant rebuff at this failure of judging the true state of things. But I was resolved to fathom the mystery somehow."

Nevertheless, the Western-philosophy based on reason, which inculcated deeply in the young person's mind that you couldn't judge the world if you lost your own identification or the I-ness, did cast a jolt by these strange experiences. Narendra, however, was still not a believer in the experience. He was still on his guard, lest like many imposters and masqueraders, he might again be taken for a ride. So he still kcpt an open mind, though gradually faith and belief were ousting rationalism and doubt. One could even doubt what one heard, however reliable be the source. One could even doubt what one saw as the mirage, or an accomplished magician tricking the eyes. But how could one doubt what he had experienced, not merely with one of the senses but with all in the five?

Nevertheless, when Naren had recovered from this extraordinary experience, Ramakrishna treated him with great kindness and love, as though Naren was a close friend of his. He kept looking after him and entertaining him in all possible ways till the end of the day. Then, Naren took his leave to go, at which the sage was greatly disheartened, and made him promise to come again as soon as possible.

On his third visit to Dakshineshwar, Naren was determind to keep wide-awake and to resist any attempt to hypnotise him or make him lose his sense. But Ramakrishna took him to the nearby garden of Jadenath Malik and thereafter they sat in his room. Soon Ramakrishna was in 'Samadhi' while Naren kept on looking at him in wonder. All of a sudden the Sage touched him, making him lose all outward consciousness. When he returned to his normal cousciousness, Naren found Ramakrishna stroking his chest. Later on, the Sage himself narrated as to how he questioned Naren in that stage and he found him giving all the details of his past lives which confirmed with whatever the sage had deciphered about his earlier lives.

This visit almost convinced Naren that Ramakrishna was no ordinary man. He began to respect him. Contrary to the teachings of the brahmans, he had now come across a guru who could command obedience and bring him closer to God. However, still Naren was determind to take nothing for granted. Being a sceptic he had little faith in the Hindu scriptures or even in God. He still lacked the spirit normally called 'Ananya Bhavo' which Lord Krishna told Arjuna (in the Gita)' by unswerving devotion, O Arjuna, I can be realised." Nevertheless, Naren had very much come upon that path of realisation.

Ramakrishna knew of the immense spiritual strength of Naren but he wanted this to be directed towards the regeneration of mankind. He didn't wish him to be a messiah of the distressed humanity. Doing good to human beings, rendering service to humanity and comforting those in sorrow or distress—that was the goal he had set for his this disciple following the message of Lord Krishna that he who works for the good of the world never perishes. The Sage had become so fond of Naren that he would be disconsolate if he didn't come to him for some time or took time to meet him. He would weep and pray to the Divine Mother to send him to Dakhineshwar "for six months I suffered great agony for him," he said." I loved him many times more than I did the other devotees" unable to bear Naren's absence he would say, 'Blessed Mother! I can't live without him". He would tell the amazed devotees: "I have wept much yet he doesn't come to me!" Then he would check his emotions and say: "Ah, an old man pining and weeping for somebody! What will people think of me? I can behave this way before you, because you all are close to me. But what would an outsider think? Often he would remember the song that Naren had sung before him [it was a Bengali song whose meaning is

Oh my mind, come!
Let's go home,
Why do you wander about in the foreign land,
In a foreign garb?
[These five elements, the objects are all inimical
None of them are your own ..... etc. etc.]

Notwithstanding Ramakrishna's deep love for Naren, others who didn't have the Sage's insight, didn't consider that lad to be so promising.In fact, as Sharadananda had mentioned in his memoirs, a neighbour of Naren thought this lad to be a spoilt child, grossly wordly and vain about his knowledge, who had scant respect for elders; insolently beating time on a kettle-drum and smoking cigars right beneath their noses! but it was only Ramakrishna who could see the flame of pure spiritualism burning behind. Once a few people, including some Brahmins and their heads, and the redoubtable Keshab Chandra Sen, were there. Ramakrishna opined about the Brahmos: "I could see knowledge in Keshab and others burning as a candle flame. But in Naren it was like the Blazing Sun." When the embarrassed brahmos protested, the sage said with a guileless smile: "How can I help saying so? I say nothing of my own accord. It is Mother who told me so and she never lies."

Getting this opinion once Naren even questioned the Sage peevishly, "How do you know that it was the divine Mother who told you so?" Continuing further in an irreverent vein, he said: "it may be that you want to behave so and put the responsibility of what you say on the Goddess. You like me and so wish to extol me. That's about all." When the sage was in a spiritual mood he would just be amused and ignore him. At other times he would be hurt and go to the Goddess with a heavy heart. But the divine Mother would tell him, "Don't listen to the boy. He will soon accept the truth."

Once when Naren didn't come to Dakshineshwar for a long time, Ramakrishna became rather restless. He knew that on Sundays Naren invariably went to attend brahmo sessions. So he went in search of Naren there. Since Keshab and other leading Brahmos had enough respect for Ramakrishna he was sure that he would receive a warm welcome. But most of the Brahmos were resentful of him as they thought he was weaning away their leaders. At the same time they were also eager to see this man from close quarters who could command so much respect of the awakened 'Bhadra lok' in general. For this was the reason that Ramakrishna's reaching the Brahmo meeting caused quite a flutter. The Sage, unmindful of the external deviations went straight to the dais and entered into Samadhi. This enhanced people's excitement but someone deliberately switched off the lights. This caused a stampede there.

Meanwhile Naren, who was present there, realised as to what could have drawn the Sage there. As the stampede started, he immediately managed to reach the dais and safely escorted the Sage back in a carriage. Later Naren spoke of the humiliation he had felt seeing Ramakrishna treated by the Brahmos so shabbily. He even spoke harshly to the Sage, telling him that he shouldn't have come there. But Ramakrishna was not concerned about what treatment he received. He was happy as he had met Naren. That was all he wanted. Seeing this, Naren went on reproaching him. He said that the Puranas contained a story about Bharat who grew so fond of a deer that ultimately he himself became a deer. So Ramakrishna should beware and stop thinking about him. But the unassuming Sage simply said: "I couldn't help seeing you. But what will happen now". Generally anxious, he went to consult the Divine Mother, as he always did in such situations. After a while the Sage came with a face radiating an unconcealed delight to exclaim

"You naughty boy! I will pay no heed to what you say. Mother says I love you because I detect Lord in you. The day I cease to detect Lord in you I would not even bear your sight."

Naren's doubts dissolved: There was a person named Pratap Chandra Hazra who used to stay in Dakshineshwar's garden. He wasn't well off, and so despite his spiritual decries he ever craved for miraculous powers but only to gain money. Although the Sage repeatedly advised him to mind his ways, he wouldn't listen. The Sage had also cautioned Naren to be careful about this person. Hazra was a non-believer and had scant belief in the miraculous powers of the saints or even in the efficacy of worship. His was totally a materialistic approach, perhaps accentuated by his penury. Naren was veering round to gradually accepting spiritual communion as a fact but the sceptic in him was still not extricated totally. One day, Naren, who was yet in the formative stage, was telling about the difficulty of believing that everything was Brahman as the Sage made him to believe. 'How can every object, the vessels, the water-pot and all be brahman? Naren said and Hazra agreed. In fact both had a hearty laugh at the very idea. All of a sudden Ramakrishna arrived and asked as to what were they talking about. And even without waiting for an answer, he touched Naren on the head and himself entered into Samadhi.

Naren, at the very touch by the Sage over his mind region, underwent a total change, as if by a miracle. He immediately began to behold everything as brahman. Narrating the effect of the sage's touch, Naren said later:

"That magic touch of the Master immediately brought about a drastic change in my mind. I was stupefied to find that there was nothing in the world but brahman! I saw God everywhere. . . in everything. I saw it quite clearly but kept silent to see if the idea would last. But that influence didn't abate in the course of the day. I returned home, but there too everything appeared to be brahman. I sat down to take my meal but found that everything I saw appeared to be brahman—the food, the plate, the bowl and everything that lay before me. I ate a morsel or two and sat still. I was startled by my mother's words: 'Why do you sit still? Finish your meal!" And I began to eat again. But all this while, whether eating or lying down, or going to college, I had the same experience and felt myself always in a sort of comatose state. While walking in the streets I noticed the cabs plying but didn't feel inclined to move out of the way, for I felt that the cabs and myself were of the same stuff. There was no sensation in my limbs which I thought were becoming paralysed. I had no satisfaction in eating and felt as if someone else was eating. Sometimes during a meal, and after a few minutes got up and began to eat again. The result would be that on some days I would be eating a lot and on others, negligibly. But it didn't cause any harm. My mother, however, became alarmed and said—there must be something wrong with me. She was even frightened that I might not survive for long . When this state altered a little, the world began to appear to me as a dream. While walking in Cornwalis Square, I would strike my head against the iron railings to see if they were real or only a dream. This state of things continued for some days. When I became normal again, I realised I must have had a glimpse of the advaita state. Then it struck me that the words of the scriptures were not false. Thenceforth I couldn't deny the conclusions of the advaita philosophy."

There is no doubt that such kind of experience is felt by only a chosen few. As Tulsidas says, "tehi Jaanan Jehi deen Janai/ Jaanat tumahai tumahi huyi jaayee" [He who knows You whom You wish to know and knowing You he becomes You Yourself]. The Gita says: "One person looks upon it [Brahman] as a marvel, another speaks of it as such, a third hears it is so, so even after hearing about it, no one whatever has known it knows it in that way." [For only rarely is its knower to be found]. It takes scores of births to realise that the whole universe is instinct with the same entity called Brahman.

The point needs a bit of elaboration. Once Einstein, the famous mathematician was asked whether he belived in God. And his answer was: "I don't know. But this much I know that there is Something that keeps this chaos in order." Who is that who makes the earth move round the Sun in a given time or makes the flowers bloom or the fruits shoot forth at trees at only a given time? Who like electricity permeates in the whole of the universe. It is difficult to answer these questions. Of course one can say it is Brahman. But how many of us can say with their personal experience?

The fact can't be denied yet it takes much to have this fact's first-hand realisation. As the famous English poet Wordsworth says: "And I have felt a presence that disturbs me with the joy of elevated thoughts; a sense sublime of something far more deeply interfused. Whose dwelling is the light of the setting suns. And the round ocean and the living air, And the blue sky, and in the mind of man." [*Tintern Abbey*]

However, despite this ineffable experience the rationalist in Naren was still not dead. He like his master believed that nothing should be taken for granted—neither a disciple's worthiness nor a guru's credibility. So while Ramakrishna kept on testing Naren's worthiness, Naren, in turn, tested his guru's spiritual assertion. Occasionally Ramakrishna would become totally indifferent to Naren but Naren would continue to come to him despite the neglect. At last when the guru asked the disciple why still he came, he said it was because he loved him and wanted to see him. He also tempted Naren with supernatural powers, which his beloved disciple refused. When the Sage told him that they would not help him to realise God, though they may be useful afterwards. "Then let me realise God first," was Naren's answer.

The Sage also encouraged his disciple to test him. There were so many so-called holy men who were nothing but imposters and tricksters. Naren thought he would first do this, and this was how he tested his guru.

One day when Ramakrishna had gone to Calcutta, Naren had a rupee coin slipped under the Sage's mattress.

Then he left for Panchawati to meditate. Ramakrishna always claimed that he detested material wealth and his hand might burn if he handled a coin. So, when Ramakrishna returned and went to his room he got up from the mattres as though he had received a shock. He was in pain but, of course, he didn't understand what caused it. He looked around as one bewildered. And all this while Naren was quietly sitting there and watching the happenings with concealed curiosity. Ramakrishna called his attendant and got the mattress be examined. The coin was eventually discovered. Naren did confess that he had placed the coin there to conduct the test, Ramakrishna smiled. This way, both the Master and the Disciple kept on testing each other and neither was found wanting.

Naren In Distress: Naren was hardly 21 when his father, Viswanath, died of a heart attack in 1884. Although his father was believed to be a rich person he was rather a spendthrift as he liked to have all good things of life. With the result, contrary to his outward style, when he died he left only debt to his inheritors. Being the eldest, the responsibility of supporting the family members fell on Naren. This was a bitter experience for Naren since he had never experienced penury in his life so far. But these unforeseen circumstances forced him to search for a job. But he didn't get any success. People who befriended his father and him in the days of prosperity now assiduously shunned him. He was tired of endlessly walking to meet potential employers and developed blisters on his feet in the strenuous but vain efforts.

One day while he was sitting exhausted with his friend and listening to a devotional song extolling the glory and greatness of Brahman, instead of reacting with his usual reverence he lapsed into a peevish mood. "All that is just lies," he blurted out. "Perhaps these are meant for those who have their bellies full and the bank balance brimming. It is actually meaningless for the starving." "This unexpected and irreverent blast was the result of a young man failing in his attempt to earn two square meals for the family. Although he was still invited to the parties thrown by rich zamindars, they were mostly indifferent to his financial distress. Except for making him sing a few devotional and touching songs, Naren was not of any importance to him. Once when his pious mother upbraided him saying,"You have been praying God ever since your childhood. But what has he done for you?" It was again during this hour of distress that Naren's faith started to waver and he went about proclaiming that God didn't exist. It began to be rumoured that Ramakrishna's favourite disciple had become an atheist. To those who came to find out, he said that the western philosophers were right. There was nothing called Brahman; there was no God. News of this, greatly exaggerated of course, reached Dakshineshwar before long. Although the Sage didn't say anything at the outset yet when one of the devotees drew his pointed attention to it, the Sage exclaimed: "Silence! you rogues. Mother has revealed that Naren could never sink so low. Don't speak about it any more, else, I'll have you thrown out of my room."

Meanwhile Naren continued to be miserable. He frantically clung to God, as to a log when thrown out of a ship. His trial—if it was that, was long and quite exhausting. But one day when his patience was all but exhausted, suddenly it was as though a veil was lifted and all his problems seemed to have been solved. Was it the Sage's grace that brought him enlightenment in that dark alley he seemed to be trapped in? There is no way of getting a confirmed answer to this question. But he did feel as if peace had suddenly descended on him. At once he seemed to be brimming with energy he had seemingly lost. In his mind he resolved to renounce the world and don the ochre robe.

As the coincidence would have it, that very day Naren heard about Ramakrishna visiting one of his devotees' place in Calcutta. He went to meet the Sage who pressed him to come to Dakshineshwar along with him. They took the carriage back, and when Naren sat in his room, Ramakrishna took his hand in his and with tears in his eyes began to sing a song whose meaning was. "I donot know if I should speak to you or not but I fear to lose you." Hearing this Naren couldn't control his tears, he shed profuse tears in that ecstatical out-burst. Ramakrishna, as usual was lost in his Samadhi. When he became normal and his one of the devotees asked as to what moved him so much, he said: "Ah, that is a secret between me and Naren." Then he sent all the others away. When he was alone with Naren, he said to his pet disciple: "I know you can never lead a wordly life. You have taken birth to do the Divine Mother's work. But stay with your family for my sake."

Naren left with a promise to return to him soon. Meanwhile, he began his quest of seeking employment again.

Although he did get a job, it was not a permanent one. He also made some money by translating books but all these attempts failed to provide any finacial security to him and to his family.

Before the Mother: Having failed in his endeavours, Naren went to Ramakrishna and requested him to pray to the Divine Mother for providing him some financial security. Ramakrishna asked him to do so himself. It was Tuesday, so he said: "This day is particularly sacred to Mother. Go and pray in the temple. I promise you that Mother will listen to your prayers and grant you whatever you want. The sage's words had given him the impression as if the Mother was not a mere idol but a live person 'who speaks and listens'. So he went with a firm resolve to make his prayer. But while on the way a strange feeling overpowered him; as if a divine intoxication possessed him. His walk became a little unsteady and a great joy filled his entire being. When he entered the temple, to his great amazement he felt that the idol was not a mere image but the goddess in person. He was so overwhelmed in the upsurge of an emotional ecstasy that he prostrated himself again and again before her. The prayer, for which he had come there vanished from his mind. And, instead, he asked for knowledge, discernment and unwavering devotion to her. "Grant me your uninterrupted Darshan O Mother!" he begged feelingly. When he returned and Ramakrishna asked him if he had prayed for getting his financial difficulties solved, Naren said he hadn't and the Sage again sent him to the temple. But again the same thing was repeated. Naren felt it was foolish to ask the Mother of the World for such petty things. As if one were to ask a

"Mighty Monarch a few pots of clay". With the result, he came back again, with his mission still unaccomplished. Ramakrishna mildly rebuked him, hearing about his failure to get the desired objective from the Mother. "What? You couldn't say a few words to the Mother about your family difficulties? Go again and this time make no mistake." Naren, then, went for a third time. But he couldn't utter a word about his financial difficulties before the Mother. In fact, feelings of shame overwhelmed him. Filled with remorse at the selfishness of his petty desires he prayed for nothing but knowledge and devotion.

Then suddenly it dawned upon him that it was the part of the test the Sage had put him to. He in reality didn't want Naren to ask for such worldly things. In a way he was demonstrating their uselessness and unimportance. However, he did feel that Naren's worry for financial security of his family was genuine, so on Naren's request he told him: "Rest assured! Your family would not suffer from the want of basic amenities."

This experience gave Naren a new thought about God. Till now he was obsessed with knowledge and impersonal aspect of God. Now he found that the images he so scorned were God too. In fact, it is faith that makes all the difference. Those who repudiated God found only stone images in his temples but those who were drunk in the nectar of faithful devotion detected a divine presence even in the stone images. In fact, this is the whole essence of the argument offered by the adherents of faith. No matter how viciously you condemn image worship, if you find your father's photograph being trampled under foot, you would feel the pinch of agony. Even though your father's photograph be just a piece of paper, it contains the image you respect in your heart. So the whole thing depends upon the view of the beholder.

Naren's this realisation made Ramakrishna the happiest person. He thought it to be the most important conversion in Naren's views. Once when Naren was asleep, the Sage told Vaikuntha Nath Sanyal, one of his disciples,: "Look at him. He felt ashamed to ask Mother for petty things. Is it not wonderful that at last he accepted Mother? "And this the Sage kept on saying again and again.

This conversion in the disciple brought him very close to his master. When Naren visited the Sage before leaving Calcutta, the former came so close to the latter as though he was lying in his disciple's lap. He pointed to himself and then to Naren and said "I am this and again that! The water on either side of a stick floating on it is really the same. There is no difference. Then he wanted to smoke and Naren filled his 'Hookkah' [hubble-bubble]. After the Sage had taken a few puffs at it, he handed it over to Naren and asked him to smoke it, while holding the pipe with his hand. Naren, naturally, hesitated. How could he have smoked a pipe which was touching the Sage's hands and lips? Won't it be tantamount to showing disrespect to his guru? But Ramakrishna insisted: "What a foolish idea," he said with perceptible annoyance. "Am I any different from you? We are one!"he again put his hand towards Naren, who then took a few puffs.

This incident shows Ramakrishna's accepting Naren as an extension of his own personality. He was actually preparing a bridge between the two so that he could transmit all that he knew to his pet disciple. Speaking of his all-encompassing love of the Sage for him, Naren remarked later on:

"Sri Ramakrishna was the only person who, ever since he had met me, believed in me uniformly throughout. Even my mother and brothers did not do so. It was his unflinching trust and love for me that bound me to him for ever. He alone knew how to love another. Worldly people only make a show of love for selfish ends." Thus Narendra Nath Dutta who was to earn global renown as Vivekananda later on, surrendered himself to the master. And Sri Ramakrishna, with infinite patience, calmed the rebellious spirit of his young disciple and led him forth from doubt to certainty and from anguish to spiritual bliss. But, more than Sri Ramakrishna's spiritual guidance and support, it was his love as Naren himself confessed—which conquered young Narendranath. And the disciple, too, returned it in equal measure. In fact, that kind of love must invoke its reciprocation. It is that pristine stream that drags out its guileless match in whoever it detects its traces. As an Urdu poet, Jigar Moradabadi claims in one of his shairs';

"Sadaaquat ho to dil seenon se
khichane lagte hain waiz!
Haqueekat khud hee manavaa deti hai
maani nahin jaati!"

[The genuineness of feeling itself attracts the hearts towards it; the vivacity need not compel you to believe it for you can't escape believing it.]

With Sri Ramakrishna's illness and his removal to Corsipore[1], on the outskirts of Calcutta for treatment, began Naren's final training under his guru. It was a remarkable time for the intense spiritual fire which burned within him and which expressed itself through various intense practices. The sage utilised the opportunity to bring his young disciple under the leadership of Naren. And when Naren asked that he might be blessed with *Nirvikalpa Samadhi*- normally regarded as the highest spiritual experience, the Sage admonished him by saying: "Shame on you! I thought you would grow, like a huge banyan, sheltering thousands from the scorching misery of the world. But now I see you seek your own liberation." All the same, Naren had the much coveted realisation, after which the Sage said that the key to this would thenceforth remain in his keeping and the door would not be opened till Naren had finished the task for which he had taken birth. Three or four days before his 'Mahasamadhi', Sri Ramakrishna transmitted to Naren his own power and told him; "By the force of the power transmitted by me, great things would be done by you only after that will you go to whence you came."

Later, when Ramakrishna was on his death-bed, doubt entered Naren's mind again whether this poor suffering man could be an incarnation of God. The sage instantly knew what he was thinking and said in a clear voice: "Aren't you convinced yet, Naren? He who was born as Rama and Krishna now abides in the body of Ramakrishna." Thus Naren at last had the Sage's own words for it. He expressly

---

1. Please read the details in our book on Swami Ramakrishna under the same series of books.

disclosed to him that he was an Avatara [God's incarnation on earth].

After the passing away of the Sage in August 1886, many of the young disciples gathered together in an old dilapidated house at Baranagore under the leadership of Naren. Here, in the midst of a life of intense austerity and spiritual practices, the foundation of the Ramakrishna brotherhood was laid. It was during these days that Naren, alongwith many of his brother disciples went to Antpur, and there on Christmas Eve (1886), sitting round a huge fire in the open, they took the vow of 'Sanyas'. Those days at Barangore were full of great joy, study, and spiritual practices. But the call of the wandering life of the 'sannyasi' was now felt by most of the monks. And Naren, too, would towards the close of 1888, began to take temporary excursions away from the math (the monastery centre). Perhaps the soul of the Sage was beckoning Naren to spread his message to the people distressed by worldly miseries. So he set about first to undertake a long visit to familiarise himself with the country of his origin.

4

The Wandering Monk

A remarkable change of outlook came in Naren between the end of 1888, when he first left on his temporary excursions and 1890, when he parted finally from his brethren and travelled alone as an unknown mendicant. He visited many places in India—Delhi, Rajputana (Rajasthan), Bombay, Poona, Kolhapur, Alwar, Mysore, Ramnad, Khetri and other places, finally reaching south to Kanya-kumari (or Cape Comorim). During his visits he met common people, maharajas, rich, poor, those starving and found India first as much a riddle then as it is now-divided between the rich and the poor; the learned and ignorant; cleanliness and filth. He was so disgusted at times that he would give a stock to people to make them come out of their disbelief and superstition. To the westernised King of Alwar who despised Indians for their image worship he gave such a shock by asking his prime minister to wrench away the ruler's painting from the wall it hung on, and spit on it. "after all it is only an inanimate object carrying your highness's image and not you yourself". He was to impress upon the bewildered king! To Brahmins who wanted him to tell them as to which was the golden period of Hindu history, he gave the shocking reply: "When five Brahmins used to devour one cow!" It was in the same vein that he "even advised Hindus to give up vegetarianism if they wished to march along with other nations of the world."

He lived in houses inhabited with prostitutes families in Tibet who practised polyandry and thought it selfish of a man to keep one woman all to himself! He even kept company with thieves, observing that sinners were saints in the making and befriended low caste people who, despite their misery, managed to repose faith in God. He was sometimes embarrassed too, as at Khetri, when a dancer appeared, he scornfully rose to leave but detained by the maharaja, heard her sing a spiritual song [penned by Surdas] which he would remember throughout his life with great reverence:

Prabhoo more avagun chita na dharo!
Samadarshee hai naam tiharo chaho to paar karo!
Ek loha pooja-ghar rakhat ek ghar badhik paro
Guru avaguna paaras nahin chitavat, kanchan karata kharo!
Ek nadiya ek naar kahavat, mailo hee neer bharo!
Jab dono mili ek baran bhaye surasari naam paro!

[O Lord! Look not on my evil qualities since you are supposed to have even view for everything. So help me go across this mudane ocean. One piece of iron in the image is the temple and another in the knife in the hand of the butcher. But when they touch the philosopher's stone, both alike turn into gold. So lord, look not on my evil qualities. One drop of water is in the sacred river and another is foul in the ditch by the roadside. But when they fall into the Ganga both alike become holy. So Lord, look not on my evil qualities since thy name is Same-sightedness].

Writing in his celebrated book 'Prophets of the New India Romain Rolland claims that the thought of going west first came to Naren between 1891 when he was visiting Junagadh and Porbandar. But before that it was the natural desire of an Indian monk to meet his country men and to assess what his country had to offer to the west. Under the influence of his burning desire to know India better, he went first to Varanasi, the holiest city of the Hindus. After Varanasi, he visited Lucknow, Agra, Vrindavan, Hathras and Rishikesh and then returned to Baranagore for a time. At Hathras, he met Sharat Chandra Gupta who became his first disciple with the name 'Swami Sadananda'. He revealed to him the mission entrusted to him by his Master, namely, the spiritual regeneration of India and the world. Sharat, who was on the staff of railway station at Hathras, resigned his post and followed the guru to help in his mission.

An important event in Naren's life at this time occurred in 1890, when he met Pavahari Baba of Ghazipur, for whose saintliness he had greatest admiration throughout his life.At this time he was torn between the desire, on one hand, to become absorbed in the eternal silence of the Absolute and, on the other, the desire of fulfil his Master's mission. He hoped that Pavahari Baba would appease the remose gnawing at his heart, which was due to the fact that the fervour for the highest absorption in the Divine drew him away from the work entrusted to him by his Master. For twenty one days, Naren was on the point of yielding to the temptation, but the vision of Sri Ramakrishna always came to draw him back.

It was in July 1890, Naren, now a Swami, took leave of Ma Sarada Devi, the holy consort of Sri Rama Krishna, who was the spiritual guide of the young monks after the Master's passing away. He also took leave of his brother monks, with the firm resolve to cut himself free from all ties and to go into the solitude of the Himalayas, for he felt it essential to be alone. In the words of Romain Rolland: "This was the great departure. Like a diver, he plunged into the Ocean of India and the Ocean of India covered his tracks. He was nothing more than one nameless, 'Sannyasin' in saffron robe among a thousand others, but the fire of genius burned in his eyes. He was a prince dispite all disguise."

His wandering took him to various places of pilgrimage and historical interest in Uttar Pradesh, Rajasthan, Gujarat, Maharashtra, Mysore, Kerala, Madras and Hyderabad. Everywhere the glory of ancient India vividly came before his eyes, whether political, cultural or spiritual. In the midst of this great education, the abject misery of the Indian masses stood out before his mind. He moved from one princely state to another, everywhere to explore avenues of mitigating their lot. Thus he came to meet many leading personalities and their rulers. Among them, Maharaj Ajit Singh of Khetri became his fast friend and ardent disciple. At Alwar, he studied the 'Mahabhashya' of Patanjali. At Poona he stayed with Bal Gangadhar Tilak, the great national leader. At first Tilak talked with the monk somewhat ironically,but later his depth of learning and profundity of thought impressed him and he invited the Swami to stay with him. From there, after a stay at Belgaum, he went to Bangalore and Mysore. The Maharaja of Mysore gave him the assurance of financial support to enable him to go to the west to seek help for India and to preach the eternal religion. From Mysore he visited Trivandrum and Kanya Kumari.

Wherever he went, it was not the important places and people that impressed him most. It was the terrible poverty and misery of the masses that caused his soul to burn in agony. He had travelled throughout India, often on foot, for nearly three years, coming to know India at first hand. Now he had reached the end of the jounery, as it were. He prostrated himself with great feeling before the image of Mother Kumari at Kanya Kumari.(Cape Coomirin) temple. Then he swam across the sea to a rock off the south coast, and sitting there for the whole night went into deep meditation. The vast panorama of his experiences during his travels passed before his mind's eye. He meditated on the past, the present and the future of India feeling what an Urdu poet described:

"Aankhon men mere kitne Zamanon ka aksa hai
Sadiyan hain mere samne lamhat ki tarah.

He then took the momentous decision to go to the West to seek help for the poor India and thus gave shape to his life's mission. The rajas of Ramnad and Khetri both had already encouraged him to go abroad, offering to bear his journey expenses. It was from them that he learnt that a Parliament of Religions was to be held in Chicago in 1893 in Commemoration of the four hundreth anniversary of Columbus's discovery of America. They wished Naren to be the Hindu delegate.

So with this decision he journeyed to Rameshwaram and Madurai. He then went on to Madras, where groups of young men, headed by Alasinga Perumal were eagerly waiting for his arrival. To them he revealed his intention of visiting America to attend the Parliament of Religions. His young disciple forthwith raised a subscription for his passage. But the Monk was still not certain that it was the Divine Mother's will that he should go, and so he asked them to give away the money to the poor. At this juncture, the Monk had a symbolic dream in which Sri Ramakrishna walked out into the sea and beckoned him to follow. This, coupled with the blessings and permission of Sri Sarada Devi, who, also, in a dream, had received Sri Ramakrishna's consent, settled the question for him, and his young friends set about collecting the necessary funds.

Then he paid a short visit to Hyderabad. But, while arrangements were being made for his journey to America, there came a sudden invitation from Maharaja of Khetri to attend celebrations in connection with the birth of his son. The Monk couldn't have refused this invitation from his ardent disciple. The Maharaja accorded him a very warm welcome and promised to help him in every possible way. And it was here, at his suggestion, that Naren assumed the name 'Vivekananda'. True to his word, the Maharaja sent his personal secretary with the Swami to equip him for the jounery and see him off at Bombay. His journey to America commenced on May 31, 1893. Before his departure he spoke to Brahmananda and Teriyananda about the reason for undertaking the jounery abroad:

"I have now travelled all over India. But alas! It was agony to me, brothers, to see with my own eyes the terrible poverty and misery of the masses, and I could not restrain my tears! It is now my firm conviction that it is futile to preach religion amongst them without first trying to remove their poverty and their sufferings. It is for this reason to find more means for the salvation of the poor in India that I am now going to America."

[as quoted in Romain Rollard's Prophets of the New India]

At the moment of departure he was a bundle of effulgent energy, clad in the robes of red silk and an ochre turban with the new name Vivekananda's meaning fully agleam at his face.

5

On the Global Stage

Travelling via China, Japan and Canada, Swami Vivekananda reached Chicago about the middle of July. He visited some Buddhist monastries at Canton; in Japan, he noted with admiration the industrial progress and cleanliness of the people. But when he reached Chicago, he was puzzled like a child seeing the city dazzling with riches and inventive genius of the West. It was here that he felt some disappointment also, knowing about the scheduled date of the Parliament of Religious which was still two months away. He was also dismayed at learning about the indispensable requirement of having authorised credentials, a necessary condition for the participating delegates. He felt lost, but resigning himself to the will of Providence, he went to Boston which was less expensive than Chicago. In the train he happened to become acquainted with Miss Katherine Sanborn, who invited to be her guest at Boston. Through her he came to know Professor John Herony Wright of Harvard University, who gave him a letter of introduction to the Chairman of the Parliament of Religion. In the course of that letter, Dr. Wright said: "Here is a man who is more learned than all our learned professors put together."

During his short stay at Boston, the lady also made him deliver lectures in a couple of churches there. He seemed to have made a good impression at his audience, as the lady wrote: "He is an educated gentleman and knows as much [about various faiths] as anybody. He has been a monk since he was eighteen. Their vows are very much more (stern) than our vows. He is wonderfully clever and clear in putting his arguments. You can't trip him up, nor get ahead of him." On his part Vivekananda admired the industry and progressiveness of the western countries and condemned the lethargy of his own. His hosts paid for his fare back to Chicago early in September and also gave him the address of the Committee which was looking after the affairs of Parliament. But Vivekananda lost the address. Reaching Chicago he slept the night through in the Railway freight yard in a box cat? Next morning he tried to find out about the Parliament, but nobody would demean to talk to a coloured man. They took him to be a negro and shunned him. After wandering fruitlessly, and tired, he sat down on the pavement. Mrs. Hale, a lady living on the other side of road, who later became his ardent follower, guessed from his clothes that he was perhaps a delegate to the Parliament of Religion. She invited him in and took him to the headquarters of the committee, "How strange are the ways of God" Vivekananda exclaimed. But since every time a lady came to guide him, it may be takes as though the Divine Mother was guiding him to his destination!

The Parliament of Religions opened on 11 September 1893. The spacious hall of the Art Institute was packed with nearly 70,000 people, representing the best culture of the country. On the platform, every organised religion from all corners of the world had its representatives. The Swami had never addressed such a huge and distinguished gathering before. He felt extremely nervous. When his turn came, he mentally bowed down to Goddess Saraswati, and then began his address with the words: "Sisters and Brothers of America!" Immediately there was a thunderous applause from the vast audience, and it lasted for a couple of minutes. It is said: "Seven thousand people rose to their feet as a tribute to something they knew not what." The appeal of his simple words of burning sincerity, his great personality, his bright countenance and his orange robe was so great that next day the newspapers described him as the greatest figure in the Parliament of Religions. The simple man with a begging bowl had become the man of the hour. In his address he spoke lucidly while expounding on the nobleness of the Vedanta, pointing out the unity of all religions, speaking not merely for his own countrymen but for all humanity.

At the end, the ovation was tremendous. It was as though the spirit of Ramakrishna was guiding him and speaking through his mouth. "Help and not fight," he exhorted everyone, "and assimilate and do not destroy; have harmony and not dissension." His fame spread like a wild-fire. The *New York Herald* wrote: "He is undoubtedly the greatest figure in the Parliament of Religions. After hearing him, we feel how foolish it is to send missionaries to this learned nation." The Committee would make him speak the last so as to keep the audience there. And people would patiently wait for hours through the stultified lectures of others to hear him speak. All the subsequent speeches of the

Swami at the Parliament were listened to with great respect and admiration.They all had one common theme - universality. While all the delegates to the Parliament spoke of thier own religion the Swami spoke of a religion that was vast as the sky and deep as the ocean. When the Parliament ended, the days of quite had ended for the Swami. What followed were days of hectic tours in almost every part of the United States. Having signed a contract for a lecture tour with a bureau, the Swami had to be constantly on the move, speaking to all sorts of audiences. Though these tours provided him with the opportunity of knowing different aspects of western life at first hand, he found that the bureau exploited and embarrassed him. He felt disgusted and severed his connexion with it. Now he wanted to form a group of earnest American disciples, and began classes, free of charge, for sincere students. His stay in the west, which lasted till December 1896, was packed with intense activity: apart from innumerable lectures and classes at New York, he founded a Vedanta Society there trained a band of close disciples at the Thousand Island Park; and he wrote the *Raja Yoga* and paid two successful visits to England where he gave the lectures which now form the book *The Gyana Yoga*. There he made some disciples, prominent among them being Capt. and Mrs. Sevier, Sister Nivedita and E.T. Sterdy. Earlier in New York, J.J. Goodwin, a young English stenographer, had been accepted as his disciple. It was during those visits that he had the pleasure of meeting the great savants Max Muller and Paul Deussen, both internationally reputed scholars of Vedanta and Hindu philosophy.

The Swami was greatly impressed by the British. In one of his letters he says: "No one ever landed on English soil with more hatred in his heart for a race than I did for the English. There is none among you (addressing his British admirers) who loves English people more than I do now." In another letter to his US disciple he wrote: "My ideas about the English have been revolutionised. [They are] a nation of heroes: the true Kshatriyas [warriors]...brave and sturdy... Their education is to hide their feelings and never to show them. But with all this heroic superstructure there is a deep spring of feeling in the Englishman's heart. If you once knew how to reach it, he is your friend for ever. If he has once the idea put into his brain, it never comes out; and the intense practicality and energy of the race makes it sprout up and immediately bear fruit. They have solved the secret of obedience without slavish cringing of great freedom with great law-abidingness."

Romain Rolland adds that Vivekananda found the English a race worthy of envy! "She forces even those whom she represses to respect her. Even those who are burning consciences of their subjected people and who wish to erase her, the Ramamohan Roys, the Vivekanandas, the Tagores, the Gandhis - are obliged to recognise the greatness of the victor, the legitimacy of the victory and perhaps even the utility of loyal collaboration with her. In any case if they had to change their conquerers they would not choose any other. With all the monstrous abuses of her domination she seems the one nation of all the west (and I include the whole of Europe and America in that term) to offer the greatest scope for free development of Indian ideas." [*Prophets of the New India*].

Vivekananda had laboured hard to give to the West his message of Vedanta as the universal principle basic to all religions, and his effort had by now resulted in the establishment of the Vedanta work on a permanent basis in the United States. The London work, too, had made some progress. Now his motherland was calling him and was eager to receive his message. So, from London, he started for India at the end of 1896. Besides his American and English disciples, he left behind his brother disciple Saradananda and Abhedananda to carry on his work.

Vivekananda's this triumphant maiden visit to the West was significant because it was for the first time the West heard someone from the land of 'snake-charmers' and 'the maharajahs' talking in terms of logic and establishing the supremacy of faith only when it grew out of the foundations of reason. India, for the first time, produced its worthy spiritual envoy to shake the world of the West based on pure reason. Vivekananda told them that reason and faith were not adversaries but indeed complementary to each other for without faith, reason is unbearable but without reason faith is unbearable. His victory news had started flooding the native country which eagerly awaited for its victorious envoy.

6

Return To India of the Triumphant Swami

It was on December 16, 1896 that Swami Vivekananda left London with the seviers and after a visit to Rome and other places in Italy, he took the boat for India at Naples on December 30. The party reached Colombo on January 15, 1897. The success in England and USA of the Swami was triumphantly and proudly acclaimed in India. The people everywhere in the country were afire with enthusiasm to receive him. Now he was no more an unknown Sannyasi but a Swami renowned even in far shores. In every city, small or big, committees had been formed to give him a rousing reception: Describing the event, Romain Rolland says: "The Swami replied to the frenzied expectancy of the people by his Message to India, a conch sounding the resurrection of the land of Rama, Shiv and Krishna, and calling the heroic spirit, the immortal Atman of March to war. He was a general, explaining his 'plan of campaign' and calling his people to rise en masse: "My India, arise! Where is your vital force? In your Immortal Soul!"

At Madras, he delivered five public lectures, each of which was a clarion call to throw away weakness and superstition and rise to build a new India. He emphasised that in India 'the key note of the whole music of the national life, was religion, a religion which preached the 'spiritual oneness of the whole universe, and when that was strengthened, everything would take care of itself. He didn't spare his criticism however, castigating his countrymen for aping the West, for their blind adherence to old superstitions, for their caste prejudices, and so on. He told his own people: "you cannot manufacture even a needle and yet you criticise the English! Fools! Learn from them their arts and industries." He didn't spare his contempt in condemning the sloth and the complacency of Indians, their self-imposed poverty and their lack of enterprise.

It was on February 20, 1897 that from Madras the Swami sailed for Calcutta. His native city gave him a grand welcome, and here the Swami paid a touching tribute to his Master, Ramakrishna: "If there has been anything achieved by me, by thoughts or words, or deeds; if from my lips had every fallen one word that has helped anyone in the world, I lay no claim to it. It was his (the Master's). If this nation wants to rise, take my words for it, it will have to rally round his name."

But despite all these enconia and praises showered on him for his winning the West, the success didn't go to his head. Humble as ever, he handed over all the money which had been given to him for building a mission in the holy memory of his Master. It was his attempt to establish his work on a firm basis. The Swami summoned all the monastic and lay disciples to a meeting at Balarama Bose's house, and the organisation called Ramakrishna Mission was formed on May 1, 1897. The aims and ideals propounded by the Swami were purely spiritual and based on humanitarian grounds. He had, in fact, inaugurated a network for carrying out his ideas which he had learnt from his Master. Since the root of the thought was given by Ramakrishna which Vivekananda had only established and enlarged to the whole world, the organisation was aptly named after the great Sage of modern India, Sri Ramakrishna Paramahansa.

The Mission started founding hospitals and helping in relief of famine. When plague broke out in Calcutta in May 1898, he organised relief work with the help of the members of the monastery and lay disciples. After the plague was under control, the Swami and his western disciples left for Nainital and Almora. This was a period of great preparation and training for his western disciples, especially sister Nivedita. On June16, the Swami left for Kashmir which was an unforgettable experience both for the Swami and his disciples. At the end of July, the Swami journeyed with sister Nivedita to the holy shrine of Amaranath. Observing meticulously every little practice demanded by custom, the Swami reached the cave of Amarnath on August 2, wearing only lioncloth, his body besmeared with ashes. His mystical experience came over him, of which he never spoke, beyond saying that "Shiv himself appeared before him." This was followed by a lonely visit to Kshir Bhavani, the shrine of the Mother Goddess, a few miles away from

Srinagar. This proved to be another memorable experience for the Swami. He was full of the Mother and said, quoting from his own poem: "If all came true, every word of it; and I have proved it, for I have hugged the form of Death."

Now the heavy toil of much wandering with no rest and very hectic schedule started taking a heavy toll on his health, with the result, when he reached Calcutta on October 18, he was pale and weak and suffering from various ailments. But neglecting all this he continued to engage himself in hectic activites. He was helpless because this was the time his dream was assuming reality. A piece of land had been acquired at Beher on the West bank of the Ganga, five miles above Calcutta, and the construction of the monastery had started. In January 1899, the monks moved in the new monastery, the now famous Beher Math. The Nivedita Girl's School had been inaugurated earlier. The Bengali monthly *Udbodhan* was also started at this time. And the Seviers fulfilled the Swami of having a monastery in the Himalaya, by starting the Advaita Ashram at Mayawati (Almora) in March 1899. The English monthly *Prabuddha Bharata* had been started at Madras earlier, but due to the untimely passing away of its editor in 1898, it ceased publication for a month. The monthly was revived again from Almora under the editorship of Swami Swaroopananda, a disciple of Swami Vivekananda, and in 1899, it was transferred to the Advaita Ashrama at Mayawati.

During this period, despite his frail health, the Swami continued to inspire the 'Sannyasis' and the 'brahmacharis' at the math towards life of intense spirituality and service, for one's own emancipation and the good of one's fellow men: *Atmano moksharthan jagat hitaya sa* as he put it.

But what was causing concern to his disciples was the Swami's failing health. It was about this time that he received an invitation to visit the West again. It was heartily welcomed by his brother monks as this could provide an ideal opportinity to improve his health as well.

7

Second Encounter With the West

Taking along Sister Nivedita and Swami Turiyamanda Swami Vivekananda left India on June 20 for his second encounter with the West. The journey with the Swami was a great experience for his two close associates. Writing about this journey, Sister Nivedita said: "From the beginning to the end, a vivid flow of stories went on. One never knew moment would bring the flash of intuition and ringing utterance of some fresh truth." After touching Madras, Colombo, Aden and Marseilles enroute the ship arrived at London on July 31. (The trip did wonders to the Swami's failing health and he looked cheerful and healthy once again.)

The party spent two weeks in London before sailing off to New York. Arriving there, he went with Mr. and Mrs. Leggett to their beautiful country home called Ridgely Manor on river Hudson. The Swami stayed at his country retreat until November 5, and then decided to visit the West coast. He visited Los Angeles, Oakland, San Francisco and also made short trips to Chicago and Detroit. Now he was convinced that the East and the West must meet since it was bound to prove mutually beneficial to both. He felt that mere material brilliance of the West couldn't dazzle him; similarly the emphasis on spirituality of the East could not hide its social and economic drawbacks. What they both needed was judicious balance of the two. He once said to Sister Nivedita: "Social life in the West is like a peal of laughter; but underneath, it was wail. It ends in a sob. Here in India it is sad and gloomy on the surface but underneath are carelessness and merriment" While the West had tried to conquer external nature, the East the internal nature. Hence East and West must work in tandem for the good of each other. Let the two meet for the benefit of entire humankind. His firm conviction was that a bridge must be formed so that the two could meet. And it was he who was laying the first pillar of that bridge.

The main achievement for him during this period was the starting of Shanti Ashrama in North California, which he placed under the charge of Swami Turiyananda. It was in his second visit to America that a Vedanta Centre was inagurated at San Francisco. He also delivered a number of lectures in the western cities during this trip. However, his health was again deteriorating and he was getting increasingly aware of his approaching end. He wrote to Miss Macleond: "My boat is nearing the calm harbour from which it is never to be driven out."

On July 20 that year he crossed the Atlantic and arrived at Paris where he had been invited to a Congress on the History of Religions, which unlike the Chicago Congress was largely about historic and scientific subjects. A charge against the Vedanta was made that the Vedic religion had its source in Nature worship. He refuted it, and clamied the Gita as the prominent source of Hindusim and its superiority over Buddhism. He appreciated the French culture and said; "Paris is the centre and the source of European cultures. She is the home of liberty, and she has infused new life into Europe." He also spent some time in London with his friends Mrs. Ole Bull and Sister Nivedita.

This time, however, he lost most of his admiration for western culture. He said: "here the fun and frivolity are on the surface, reality is full of tragic intensity.' In his first visit he had been struck by the progress and modernisation he saw in the West. Now he had a closer look and saw the ills of the progress—the race for money and wealth; the ogre of materialism behind the veil of affluence. He found the two things which his guru had repeatedly condemned - Kamini and Kanchan [lust for sensual pleasure and wealth] most sought after. Vienna, Constantinople, Turkey, Greece and finally Egypt—such was the itinery of his jounery back.

At Egypt, he suddenly felt his work was done in the West and he took the first boat going homewards. While in Cairo he had a premonition of Capt. Sevier's death. He hurried back to India and reached the Beher Math on December 9, 1900, without any previous intuition. It was a pleasant surprise to his brother monks and disciples who greatly rejoiced his return. Though happy at his return to his homeland he started having premonition about his own end as he found his old friend Capt. Sevier no more.

8

The End of the Journey

It was after his arrival at Beher Math that he learnt that Capt. Sevier had passed away on October 28. So he immediately left for Mayawati (Almora) to console Mrs. Sevier. Arriving there on January 3, 1901, he stayed there for a fortnight. The grandeur of the scenery of this Himalayan Ashrama, dedicated to Advaita, delighted him. Inspite of his ill health and the severe cold, he wandered in the woods and around an artificial lake, happy and carefree.

Then after he returned to Beher and stayed there for seven weeks. After seeing the Mission functioning smoothly he left for East Bengal and Assam. His mother, who had expressed an earnest desire to visit the holy places there went with him. "This is the one great wish of a Hindu widow," he wrote to Mrs. Bull, "I have brought only misery to my people. Now I am trying to fulfil this one wish of hers: He returned to the Math in the second week of May 1901, after visiting Nangalbandha, Kamakhya and Shillong during the tour, and delivering a few lectures at Dhaka and Shillong.

Now the Swami, conscious perhaps, of his destiny, tried to lead a carefree life at the monastery. He would roam about the Math grounds, sometimes clad only in his loin-cloth; or sit with the monks singing devotional songs. Sometimes, he would be seen imparting spiritual instructions to the visitors; at other times engaged in serious study in his room or explaining to the members of the Math the intricate passage from the scriptures and unfolding to them his schemes for future work. He freed himself entirely from all formal duties by executing a Deed of Trust in favour of his brother disciples, transfering to them all the properties, including Beher Math, so far held in his name.

Towards the end of 1901, two learned Buddhists came from Japan to invite him to attend the forth coming Congress of Religions there. The Swami could not accept their invitation, but went with them to Bodh Gaya and from there to Varanasi. At Varanasi he was delighted to see a few youngmen who, under the inspiration of his message, had started nursing the poor and the needy. Their work formed the nucleus of the future Ramakrishna Mission Home of Service.

But now the Swami could feel his end was round the corner. All his actions during the last days were deliberate and significant. He said that smaller plants cannot grow under the shade of a big tree.

On July 4, 1902, a Friday he was more active and cheerful than ever before. He meditated for about three to four hours and sang a beautiful hymn to the Goddess Kali. Eating his meal heartily with his disciples, he walked along the Beher road for more than two miles, talking about Vedic studies and a scheme for a college to teach the Vedanta. He talked quite affectionately to his brother monks on many matters. "India is immortal", "he said,"if she persists in her search for God. But if she opts for politics and social dissensions, she will perish.'At seven after the evening worship, he went to his room. Looking out of his window towards the holy Ganga, he meditated for about 45 minutes. Then he opened wide all the doors and windows and called in his monks. He was lying quitely on the floor, motionless, and apparently in deep meditation. After an hour he turned around: a deep breath; his eyes fixed in the middle of his brows- the classical Yoga posture. Another deep sigh and then total silence! "There was," an eye-witness says, "some blood in his nostrils, about his mouth and in his eyes." The doctors who came after, tried artificial respirators. But it was too late.They gave the cause of death as heart failure. But Vivekananda's brother monks never for a moment doubted that he had, as Ramakrishna had said, accomplished his work and gone back where he came from. For long back, before he became Vivekananda from Naren, the Sage (Rama krishna) had said with tears in his eyes; "Today I give you all I have. You will do great good in the world through these powers, and when your work is done you will return where you came from." And so the blessed disciple of his Master completed the task assigned to him and left, to be again close to his Master. He merged into him again like a ripple merges into the river and the wave into the sea.

Although different from his Master in almost every way- physique, nature, outlook and beliefs, they were really one from the point of view of the inner convictions. As the Sage had often said: "There can be nothing more unlike each other than the flower to the leaf, yet they get their sustenance from the same tree." Vivekananda's main emphasis was on bringing peace and comfort to tortured souls, wherever they were or whatever race or nationality and in whatever circumstance. He recognised suffering as the Buddha did, and felt there was an immediate need to remove it. He sacrificed everything to end it. Speaking to monks at Beher he said: "If there is a conflict between your brain and your heart, listen to the voice of your heart." He was one to whom the sufferings of mankind were his own because he saw the same soul existing in all human beings - 'YO MAM PASHYATI' as the Gita says. He felt pain when he saw misery of the east and cold and feelingless attitude of the west. He was what an Urdu Shair 'Ameer' says in one of his shers:

Khanjar Chale Kisee pe
tadapte hain hum Ameer
Sare Jahan ka dard
hamare Jigar mein hai'

Vivekananda was no academic philosopher, nor indeed one who believed in mere renunciation. In the spirit of the Gita, he believed in the active participation in virtuous works. The Gita says: "Both renouncing work and doing them selflessly lead to the soul's emancipation, but the selfless performance of works is better of the two." Once while feasting the poor Vivekananda had confided in one of his disciples: "Sometimes I feel like throwing away all the things used for worship, cease building monasteries and so forth, and use the money to assuage the misery of the poor and hungry people". He was a 'Karma Yogi', in the true sense of the term: He had quit his mortal coil but his words uttered in 1896 to Mr. Eric Hammond in London remain to reassure everyone of his immortality. "It may be that I shall find it to get out side my body to cast it off like a wornout garment. But I shall not cease to work. I shall inspire men everywhere until the world shall know that it is one with God."

9

Views And Thoughts of Vivekananda

Swami Vivekananda had not written any autobiographical book to convey his thoughts; he was a prolific speaker. He spoke on various subjects and conveyed his message through many speeches and lectures that he delivered inside the country and abroad. All of them have been compiled in a series of books entitled: *The Complete Works of Swami Vivekananda* running into eight volumes and published by Ramakrishna Mission's Advaita Ashrama. He was an original thinker and a great visionary that India produced. For the benefit of our readers we have called his views and thoughts under the appropriate headings which are being given below.

(I) Faith and Strength

He is an atheist who does not believe in himself. The old religions said that he was an atheist who did not believe in God. The new religion says that he is an atheist who does not believe in himself. (II. 301)

The history of the world is the history of a few men who had faith in themselves. That faith calls out the divinity within. You can do anything. You fail only when you do not strive sufficiently to manifest power. As soon as a man or a nation loses faith, death comes. (VIII. 228)

Faith, faith, faith in ourselves, faith, faith in God, this is the secret of greatness. If you have faith in all the three hundred and thirty millions of your mythological gods and in all the gods which foreigners have now and again introduced into your midst, and still have no faith in yourselves, there is no salvation for you. (III. 190)

Never think there is anything impossible for the soul. It is the greatest heresy to think so. If there is sin, this is the only sin—to say that you are weak, or others are weak (II. 308)

Whatever you think, that you will be. If you think yourselves weak, weak you will be; if you think yourselves strong, strong you will be (III. 130)

Be free; hope for nothing from any one. I am sure if you look back upon your lives, you will find that you were always vainly trying to get help from others, which never came. All the help that has come was from within yourselves. (II. 324)

Never say, 'No; never say, 'I cannot', for you are infinite. Even time and space are as nothing compared with your nature. You can do anything and everything, you are almighty. (II. 300)

Ye are the children of God, the sharers of immortal bliss, holy and perfect beings. Ye divinities on earth- sinners! It is sin to call a man so; it is a standing libel on human nature. Come up, O lions, and shake off the delusion that you are sheep; you are souls immortal, spirits free, blest and eternal. (I. 11)

Never mind the struggles, the mistakes. I never heard a cow tell a lie, but it is only a cow—never a man. So never mind these failures, these little backslidings; hold the ideal a thousand times; and if you fail a thousand times make the attempt once more. (II. 152)

The remedy for weakness is not brooding over weakness, but thinking of strength. Teach men of the strength that is already within them. (II.300)

If there is one word that you find coming like a bomb from the Upanisads, bursting like a bomb-shell upon masses of ignorance, it is the word, *fearlessness*. (III. 160)

If you look, you will find that I have never quoted anything but the Upanishads. And of the Upanishads, it is only that one idea *strength*. The quintessence of the Vedas and Vedanta and all lies in that one word. (VIII. 267)

Be strong, my young friends, that is my advice to you. You will be nearer to heaven through football than through the study of the *Gita*. These are bold words, but I have to say them, for I love you. I know where the shoe pinches. I have gained a little experience. You will understand the *Gita* better with your biceps, your muscles, a little stronger. (III. 242)

This is the one question I put to every man. ....Are you strong? Do you feel strength?—for I know it is truth alone that gives strength. .... Strength is the medicine for the world's disease. (II. 201).

This is the great fact: Strength is life; weakness is death. Strength is felicity, life eternal, immortal; weakness is constant strain and misery, weakness is death. (II.3)

To succeed, you must have tremendous perseverance, tremendous will. 'I will drink the ocean', says the persevering soul, 'at my will, mountains will crumble up.' Have that sort of energy, that sort of will to work hard, and you will reach the goal (I. 178).

Men, men, these are wanted: everything else will be ready, but strong, vigorous, believing young men, sincere to the backbone, are wanted. A hundred such and the world becomes revolutionized. (III. 223-24)

Are not drums made in the country? Are not trumpets and kettle-drums available in India? Make the boys hear the deep-toned sound of these instruments. Hearing from boyhood the sound of these effeminate forms of music, ... the country is well-nigh converted into a country of women. (VII. 232)

Death is better than a vegetating ignorant life; it is better to die on the battle-field than to live a life of defeat. (II, 124).

Come, do something heroic. Brother, what if you do not attain *mukti*, what if you suffer damnation a few times? Is the saying untrue: 'There are some saints who, full of holiness in thought, word, and deed, please the whole world by their numerous beneficent acts, and who develop their own hearts by magnifying an atom of virtue in others as if it were as great as a mountain'? (VI. 314-15)

Can anything be done unless everybody exerts himself to his utmost? 'It is the man of action, the lion-heart, that the Goddess of Wealth resorts to.' No need of looking behind. FORWARD! We want infinite energy, infinite zeal, infinite courage, and infinite patience, then only will great things be achieved. (VI. 383-84).

Be not in despair; the way is very difficult, like walking on the edge of a razor; yet despair not, arise, awake, and find the ideal, the goal. (II. 124)

Why weepest thou, brother? There is neither death nor disease for thee. Why weepest thou, brother? There is neither misery nor misfortune for thee. Why weepest thou, brother? Neither change nor death was predicated of thee. Thou art Existence Absolute. ... Be your own self. (V. 275)

Let people say whatever they like, stick to your own convictions, and rest assured, the world will be at your feet. They say, 'Have faith in this fellow or that fellow', but I say, 'have faith in yourself first' that's the way. have faith in yourself-all power is in you-be conscious and bring it out. Say, 'I can do everything'. 'Even the poison of a snake is powerless, if you can firmly deny it.' (VI. 274)

Once when I was in Varansai, I was passing through a place where there was a large tank of water on one side and a high wall on the other. It was in the grounds where there were many monkeys. The monkeys of Varanasi are huge brutes and are sometimes surly. They now took it into their heads not to allow me to pass through their street, so they howled and shrieked and clutched at my feet as I passed. As they pressed closer, I began to run, but the faster I ran, the faster came the monkeys, and they began to bite at me. It seemed impossible to escape, but just then I met a stranger who called out to me, 'Face the brutes'. I turned and faced the monkeys, and they fell back and finally fled. That is the lesson for all life—face the terrible, face it boldly. (I. 338)

Stand up and fight! Not one step back, that is the idea. Fight it out, whatever comes. Let the stars move from the spheres! Let the whole world stand against us! Death means only a change of garment. What of it? Thus fight! You gain nothing by becoming cowards. Taking a step backward, you do not avoid any misfortune. You have cried to all the gods in the world. Has misery ceased?... The gods come to help you when you have succeeded. So what is the use? Die game. You are infinite, deathless, birthless. Because you are infinite spirit, it does not befit you to be a slave. Arise! Awake! Stand up and fight! (I. 461)

(II) Powers of The Mind

Take up one idea. Make that one idea your life—think of it, dream of it, live on that idea. Let the brain, muscles, nerves, every part of your body, be full of that idea, and just leave every other idea alone. This is the way to success . . . If we really want to be blessed, and make others blessed, we must go deeper. (I. 177)

All the great prophets, saints, and seers of the world—what did they do? In one span of life, they lived the whole life of humanity, traversed the whole length of time that it takes ordinary humanity to come to perfection. In one life, they perfect themselves; they have no thought for anything else, never live a moment for any other idea, and thus the way is shortened for them. This is what is meant by concentration, intensifying the power of assimilation, thus shortening the time. (I. 157)

The more this power of concentration, the more knowledge is acquired, because this is the one and only method of acquiring knowledge. Even the lowest shoeblack, if he gives more concentration, will black shoes better; the cook with concentration will cook a meal all the better. In making money, or in worshipping God, or in doing anything, the stronger the power of concentration, the better will that thing be done. This is the one call, the one knock, which opens the gates of nature, and lets out floods of light. (II. 391)

How has all the knowledge in the world been gained but by the concentration of the powers of the mind? The world is ready to give up its secrets, if we only know how to knock, how to give it the necessary blow. The strength and force of the blow come through concentration. There is no limit to the power of the human mind. The more concentrated it is, the more power is brought to bear on one point; that is the secret. (I. 130-31)

No force can be created; it can only be directed. Therefore, we must learn to control the grand powers that are already in our hands, and by will power make them spiritual, instead of merely animal. Thus it is clearly seen that chastity is the cornerstone of all morality and of all religion. (VIII. 46)

Free! We who cannot, for a moment, govern our own minds, nay, cannot hold our minds on a subject, focus it on a point to the exclusion of everything else, for a moment! Yet we call ourselves free. Think of it!... The mind uncontrolled and unguided will drag us down, down, for ever—rend us, kill us; and the mind controlled and guided will save us, free us. (VI. 30)

The main difference between men and the animals is the difference in their power of concentration. All success in any line of work is the result of this. The difference in their power of concentration also constitutes the difference between man and man. Compare the lowest with the highest man. The difference is in the degree of concentration. (VI. 37)

Ninety per cent of thought-force is wasted by the ordinary human being, and therefore, he is constantly committing blunders; the trained man or mind never makes a mistake. (VI. 123-24)

What work do you expect from men of little hearts? Nothing in the world! You must have an iron will if you would cross the ocean. You must be strong enough to pierce mountains. (VI. 297)

Good and evil thoughts are each a potent power, and they fill the universe. As vibration continues, so thought remains in the form of thought until translated into action. For example, force is latent in the man's arm until he strikes a blow, when he translates it into activity. We are the heirs of good and evil thought. If we make ourselves pure and the instruments of good thoughts, these will enter us. The good soul will not be receptive to evil thoughts. (VI. 134)

In the history of mankind, you will find that there come the Messengers, and that from their very birth their mission is found and formed. The whole plan is there, laid down; and you see them swerving not one inch from that. Because they come with a mission, they come with a message... When they speak, each word is direct; it bursts like a bomb-shell. What is in the word, unless it has the Power behind? What matters is what language you speak, and how you arrange your language? What matters is whether you speak correct grammar or with fine rhetoric? What matters if whether your language is ornamental or not? The question is: Whether or not you have anything to give? It is a question of giving and taking, and not listening. Have you anything to give?—that is the first question. If you have, then give. (IV.122-24)

Whatever you do, devote your whole mind, heart, and soul to it. I once met a great *sannyasin*, who cleansed his brass cooking utensils, making them shine like gold, with as much care and attention as he bestowed on his worship and meditation (*Life of Swami Vivekananda,* p. 284)

How to attain purity living this life? Shall we all go to the forest caves? What good would it do? If the mind is not under control, it is no use living in a cave because the same mind will bring all disturbances there. We will find twenty devils in the cave because all the devils are in the mind. If the mind is under control, we can have the cave anywhere, wherever we are.

It is our own mental attitude which makes the world what it is for us. Our thoughts make things beautiful, our thoughts make things ugly. The whole world is in our own minds. Learn to see things in the proper light. (I. 440-41)

(III) Education And Society

Education is the manifestation of the perfection already in man. (IV. 358)

What is education? Is it book-learning? No. Is it diverse knowledge? Not even that. The training by which the current and become fruitful is called education. (VI. 490)

To me the very essence of education is concentration of mind, not the collecting facts. If I had to do my education over again, and had any voice in the matter, I would not study facts at all. I would develop the power of concentration and detachment, and then with a perfect instrument I could collect facts at will. (VI. 38-39)

The education which does not help the common mass of people to equip themselves for the struggle for life, which does not bring out strength of character, a spirit of philanthropy, and the courage of a lion—is it worth the name? Real education is that which enables one to stand on his own legs. (VII. 147-48)

Education is not the amount of information that is put into your brain and runs riot there, undigested all your life. We must have life building, man-making, character-making, assimilation of ideas. If you have assimilated five ideas and made them your life and character, you have more education than any man who has got by heart a whole library. (III. 302)

Knowledge is inherent in man; no knowledge comes from outside; it is all inside... We say Newton discovered gravitation. Was it sitting anywhere in a corner waiting for him? It was in his own mind; the time came and he found it out. All knowledge that the world has ever received comes from the mind; the infinite library of the universe is in your own mind. The external world is simply the suggestion, the occasion, which sets you to study your own mind. (I. 28)

Every one wants to command, and no one wants to obey; and this is owing to the absence of that wonderful *brahmacarya* system of yore. First, learn to obey. The command will come by itself. Always first learn to be a servant, and then you will be fit to be a master. (III. 134-35)

Education, education , education! Travelling through many cities of Europen and observing in them the comforts and education of even the poor people, there was brought to my mind the state of our own poor people, and I used to shed tears. What made the difference? Education was the answer I got. (IV. 483)

What we want is this *sraddha*. Unfortunately, it has nearly vanished from India, and this is why we are in our present state. What makes the difference between man and man is the difference in this *sraddha* and nothing else. What makes one man great and another weak and low is this *sraddha*. (III. 319)

Give up the awful disease that is creeping into our national blood, that idea of ridiculing everything— that loss of seriousness. Give that up. Be strong and have this *sraddha*, and everything else is bound to follow. (III. 320)

The only service to be done for our lower classes is to give them education, *to develop their lost individuality* . . . Give them ideas—that is the only help they require, and then the rest must follow as the effect. Ours is to put the chemicals together, the crystallization comes in the law of nature . . . Now if the mountain does not come to Mohammed, Mohammed must go to the mountain. If the poor boy cannot come to education, education must to go him. (IV. 362-63)

We want that education by which character is formed, strength of mind is increased, the intellect is expanded, and by which one can stand on one's own feet. (V. 342)

Is that education, as a result of which the will, being continuously choked by force through generations, is now well-nigh killed out; under whose sway, why mention new ideas, even the old are disappearing one by one; is that education which is slowly making man a machine? It is more blessed, in my opinion, even to go wrong, impelled by one's free will and intelligence, than to be goods as an automaton. (IV. 490)

What we want are western science coupled with Vedanta, *brahmacarya* as the guiding motto, and also *sraddha* and faith in one's own self . . . . Vedanta says that within man is all knowledge—even in a boy it is so—and it requires only an awakening, and that much is the work of a teacher . . . But the root is religion. Religion is as the rice, and everything else, like the curries. Taking only curries causes indigestion, and so is the case with taking rice alone. (V. 366)

Do you see, simply by the observance of strict *brahmacarya* (continence), all learning can be mastered in a very short time—one has an unfailing memory of what one hears or knows but once. It is owing to this want of continence that everything is on the brink of ruin in our country. (VII. 224)

My idea of education is personal contact with teacher-*gurugrha-vasa*. Without the personal life of a teacher, there would be no education. Take your universities. What have they done during the fifty years (this was told at Madras in 1897)of their existence? They have not produced one original man. They are merely an examining body. The idea of the sacrifice for the common weal is not yet developed in our nation. (V.224)

Truth does not pay homage to any society, ancient and modern. Society has to pay homage to Truth or die. Societies should be moulded upon truth, and truth has not to adjust itself to society . . . . *That society is the greatest, where the highest truths become practical.* That is my opinion; and if society is not fit for the highest truth, make it so; and the sooner, the better. (II.84-85)

I say, liberate, undo the shackles of people as much as you can. When you would be able to sacrifice all desire for happiness for the sake of society, then you would be the Buddha, then you would be free. (IV. 491)

Three things are necessary to make every man great, every nation great:

1. Conviction of the powers of goodness.

2. Absence of jealousy and suspicion.

3. Helping all who are trying to be and do good. (VIII.299)

If your ideal is matter, matter shalt thou be. Behold! Our ideal is the Spirit. That alone exists. Nothing else exists, and like Him, we live for ever. (VIII. 72)

The Hindu man drinks religiously, sleeps religiously, walks religiously, marries religiously, robs religiously... Each nation has a mission for the world, so long as that mission is not hurt, that nation lives, despite every difficulty. But as soon as its mission is destroyed, the nation collapses. (VIII. 74-75)

Do you not find in history that the first death sign of a nation has been unchastity? When that has entered, the end of the race is in sight. (II. 101)

Now we are not much more moral than the animals. We are only held down by the whips of society. If society said today, 'I will not punish you if you steal', we should just make a rush for each other's property. It is the policeman that makes us moral. It is social opinion that makes us moral, and really, we are little better than animals. (II. 164)

The majority of sects will be transient, and last only as bubbles, because the leaders are not usually men of character. Perfect love, the heart never reacting, this is what builds character. There is no allegiance possible where there is no character in the leader, and perfect purity ensures the most lasting allegiance and confidence. Take up an idea, devote yourself to it, struggle on in patience, and the sun will rise for you. (VI. 135)

We are asked: What good is your Religion to society? Society is made a test of truth. Now this is very illogical. Society is only a stage of growth through which we are passing.

...If the social state were permanent, it would be the same as if the baby remained a baby. There can be no perfect man-baby; the works are a contradiction in terms, so there can be no perfect society. Man must and will grow out of such early stages... My Master used to say, 'Why don't you help your own lotus flower to bloom? The bees will then come of themselves.' (VI. 144)

Do not recognize wickedness in others. Wickedness is ignorance, weakness. What is the good of telling people they are weak? Criticism and destruction are of no avail. We must give them something higher; tell them of their own glorious nature, their birthright. (VI. 141-42)

What I say is not 'Reform', but 'Move on'. Nothing is too bad to reform. Adaptability is the whole mystery of life—the principle underneath, which serves to unfold it. Adjustment or adaptation is the outcome of the self pitted against external forces tending to suppress it. Even if I do not preach this, society is changing, it must change. (VI. 110)

Nothing else is necessary but these—*love*, *sincerity*, and *patience*. What is life but growth, i.e. expansion, i.e. love. Therefore, all love is life, it is the only law of life, all selfishness is death, and this is true here or hereafter. It is life to do good, it is death not to do good to others. Ninety per cent of human brutes you see are dead, are ghosts-for none lives, my boys, but he who loves. (IV. 367)

On one side, new India is saying, 'If we only adopt western ideas, western language, western food, western dress, and western manners, we shall be as strong and powerful as the western nation'; on the other, old India is saying, 'Fools! By imitation, others' ideas never become one's own; nothing, unless earned, is your own. Does the ass in the lion's skin become the lion?'

On one side, new India is saying, 'What the western nations do is surely good, otherwise, how did they become so great?' On the other side, old India is saying, 'The flash of lighting is intensely bright, but only for a moment; look out boys, it is dazzling your eyes. Beware!' (IV. 477)

Social life in the West is like a peal of laughter; but underneath, it is a wail. It ends in a sob. The fun and frivolity are all on the surface: really it is full of tragic intensity. Now here, it is sad and gloomy on the outside, but underneath are carelessness and merriment. (VIII. 261-62)

As far back as the days of the Upanisads, we have thrown the challenge to the world: 'Not, by progeny, not by wealth, but by renunciation alone immortality is reached.' Race after race has taken the challenge up and tried their utmost to solve the world-riddle on the plane of desires. They have all failed in the past—the old ones have become extinct under the weight of wickedness and misery, which lust for power and gold brings in its train, and the new ones are tottering to their fall. The question has yet to be decided whether peace will survive or war; whether patience will survive or non-forbearance; whether goodness will survive or wickedness; whether muscle will survive or brain; whether worldliness will survive or spirituality. We have solved our problem ages ago... Our solution is unworldliness—renunciation. (IV. 314-15)

(IV) Serve Man As God

One of the greatest lessons I have learned in my life is to pay as much attention to the means of work as to its end.... I have been always learning great lessons from that one principle, and it appears to me that all the secret of success is there: to pay as much attention to the means as to the end. (II. 1)

Our duty to others; doing good to the world. Why should we do good to the world? Apparently to help the world, but really to help ourselves.... Do not stand on a high pedestal and take five cents on your hand and say, 'Here, my poor man,' but be grateful that the poor man is there, so that by making a gift to him, you are able to help yourself. It is not the receiver that is blessed, but it is the giver. Be thankful that you are allowed to exercise your power of benevolence and mercy in the world, and thus become pure and perfect. (I. 75-76)

It is the level-headed man, the calm man, of good judgment and cool nerves, of great sympathy and love, who does good work and so does good to himself. (I. 79)

Great work requires great and persistent effort for a long time. Neither need we trouble ourselves, if a few fail.

It is in the nature of things that many should fall, that trouble should come, that tremendous difficulties should arise, that selfishness and all the other devils in the human heart should struggle hard, when they are about to be driven out by the fire of spirituality. (VIII. 382)

In doing evil, we injure ourselves and others also. In doing good, we do good to ourselves and to others as well... According to *Karmayoga*, the action one has done cannot be destroyed until it has borne its fruit; no power in nature can stop it from yielding its results. If I do an evil action, I must suffer for it; there in no power in this universe to stop or stay it. Similarly, if I do a good action, there is no power in the universe which can stop its bearing good results. (I.82)

The watchword of all well-being, of all moral good, is not 'I' but 'Thou'. Who cares whether there is a heaven or a hell, who cares if there is a soul or not, who cares if there is an unchangeable or not? Here is the world, and it is full of misery. Go out into it as Buddha did not struggle to lessen it or die in the attempt. Forget yourselves; this is the first lesson to be learnt, whether you are a theist or an atheist, whether you are an agnostic or a *Vedantist*, a Christian or a Mohammedan. (II. 353)

Buddha is the only prophet who said, 'I do not know your various theories about God. What is the use of discussing all the subtle doctrines about the soul? Do good and be good. And this will take you to freedom and to whatever truth there is.'... he works best who works without any motive, neither for money, nor for fame, nor for anything else; and when a man can do that, he will be a Buddha, and out of him will come the power to work in such a manner as will transform the world. (I. 117-18)

Selfishness is the chief sin, thinking of ourselves first. He who thinks, 'I will eat first, I will have more money than others, and I will possess everything,' he who thinks, 'I will get to heaven before others, I will get *mukti* before others;, is the selfish man. The unselfish man says, 'I will be last, I do not care to go to heaven, I will even go to hell, if by doing so I can help my brothers,' This unselfishness is the test of religion. He who has more of this unselfishness is more spiritual and nearer to Siva. (III. 143)

You cannot help anyone, you can only serve; serve the children of the Lord, serve the Lord Himself, it is you who have the privilege. If the Lord grants that you can help any one of His children, blessed you are; do not think too much of yourselves. Blessed you are that that privilege was given to you when others had it not. Do it only as a worship. (III. 246)

Blessed are we that we are given the privilege of working for Him, not of helping Him. Cut out this word 'help' from your mind. You cannot help; it is blaspheming. You are here yourself at His pleasure. Do you mean to say, you help Him? You worship. When you give a morsel of food to the dog, you worship the dog as God. God is in that dog. He is all and in all. (V. 246)

After so much austerity, I have understood this as the real truth—God is present in every *jiva*; there is no other God besides that. 'Who serves *jiva*, serves God indeed.' (VII. 247)

If in this hell of a world, one can bring a little joy and peace even for a day into the heart of a single person, that much alone is true; this I have learnt after suffering all my life; all else is mere moonshine. (V. 176)

One idea that I see clear as daylight is that misery is caused by *ignorance* and nothing else. Who will give the world light? Sacrifice in the past has been the Law, it will be, alas, for ages to come. The earth's bravest and best will have to sacrifice themselves for the good of many, for the welfare of all. Buddhas by the hundred are necessary with eternal love and pity. (VIII. 498)

Let us calmly and in a manly fashion go to work, instead of dissipating our energy in unnecessary frettings and fumings. I, for one, thoroughly believe that no power in the universe can withhold from anyone anything he really deserves. The past was great no doubt, but sincerely believe that the future will be more glorious still. (IV. 366)

Behold, how men are already in the jaws of the shark of infatuation! Oh, listen to their piteous heart-rending wails. Advance! Forward! O ye brave souls, to set free those that are in fetters, to lessen the burden of woe of the miserable, and to illumine the abysmal darkness of ignorant hearts. Look, how the Vedanta proclaims by beat of drums, 'Be fearless!' (VII. 500-01)

The only way of getting our divine nature manifested is by helping others to do the same. If there is inequality in nature, still there must be equal chance for all—or if greater for some and for some less—the weaker should be given more chance than the strong. In other words, a *Brahmana* is not so much in need of education as a *Candala*. If the son of a *Brahmana* needs one teacher, that of a *Candala*, needs ten. For greater help must be given to him whom nature has not endowed with an acute intellect from birth. It is a madman who carries coals to Newcastle. The poor, the downtrodden, the ignorant—let these be your god. (VI. 319)

This is the gist of all worship—to be pure and to do good to others. He who sees *Siva* in the poor, in the weak, and in the diseased, really worships *Siva*; and if he sees *Siva* only in the image, his worship is but preliminary. (III. 141-42)

The life of Buddha shows that even a man who does not believe in God, has no metaphysics, belongs to no sect, and does not go to any church, or temple, and is a confessed materialist, even he can attain to the highest....he was the only man who was ever ready to give up his life for animals, to stop a sacrifice. He once said to a king: 'If the sacrifice of a lamb helps you to go to heaven, sacrificing a man will help you better; so sacrifice me.' The king was astonished. (IV. 136)

'The good live for others alone. The wise man should sacrifice himself for others.' I can secure my own good only by doing your good. There is no other way, none whatsoever. (VI. 317)

Go from village to village, do good to humanity and to the world at large. Go to hell yourself to buy salvation for others...'When death is so certain, it is better to die for a good cause.' (VI. 265-67)

Throughout the history of the world, you find great men make great sacrifices and the mass of mankind enjoy the benefit. If you want to give up everything for your own salvation, it is nothing. Do you want to forgo even your own salvation for the good of the world? You are God, think of that.(VI. 280)

This world is not for cowards. Do not try to fly. Look not for success or failure. Join yourself to the perfectly unselfish will and work on. Know that the mind which is born to succeed joins to a determined will and perseveres... Live in the midst of the battle of life. Anyone can keep calm in a cave or when asleep. Stand in the whirl and madness of action and reach the Centre. If you have found the centre, you cannot be moved. (VI. 83-84)

A hundred thousand men and women, fired with the zeal of holiness, fortified with eternal faith in the Lord and nerved to lion's courage by their sympathy for the poor and the fallen and the downtrodden, will go over the length and breadth of the land, preaching the gospel of social raising-up—the gospel of equality. (V. 15)

My boy, if you have any respect for my words, the first thing I will advise you to do is to throw open all the doors and windows of your room. In your quarter there are lots of poor people sunk in degradation and misery. You will have to go to them and serve them with your zeal and enthusiasm. Arrange to distribute medicines to those who are sick, and nurse them with all care, supply food to him who is starving, teach with as much as lies in you the ignorant; and if you begin to serve your brethren in this wise, I tell you, my child, you will surely get peace and consolation. (*Reminiscences of Swami Vivekananda,* p.330)

Where is that martial spirit which, at the very outset, requires one to know how to serve and obey, and to practice self-restraint? The martial spirit is not-self-assertion, but self sacrifice. One must be ready to advance and lay down one's life at the word of command, before he can command the hearts and lives to others. One must sacrifice himself first. (VII. 270)

It is fear alone that is death. You have to go beyond all fear. So from this day, be fearless. Off at once, to lay down your life for your own liberation and for the good of others. What good is it carrying along a load of bones and flesh! (VI. 473)

Trust not to the so-called rich, they are more dead than alive. The hope lies in you—in the meek, the lowly, but the faithful. Have faith in the Lord; no policy, it is nothing. Feel for the miserable and look up for help—it *shall come*... I may perish of cold or hunger in this land, but I bequeath to you, young men, this sympathy, this struggle for the poor, the ignorant, the oppressed.... Vow, then, to devote your whole lives to the cause of the redemption of these three hundred millions, going down and down every day. (V. 16-17)

The history of the world is that of six men of faith, six men of deep pure character. We need to have three things: the heart to feel, the brain to conceive, the hand to work. Make yourself a dynamo. *Feel* first for the world. ...Ask yourself, does your mind react in hatred or jealousy? Good works are continually being undone by the tons of hatred and anger which are being poured out on the world. If you are pure, if you are strong, *you one* man, are equal to the whole world. (VI. 144-45)

Will such a day come when this life will go for the sake of others' good? The world is not a child's play-and great men are those who build highways for others with their heart's blood. This has been taking place through eternity, that one builds a bridge by laying down his own body, and thousands of others cross the river through its help. Be it so! Be it so! (VI. 273-74)

(V) Religion and Ethics

Religion is the idea which is raising the brute unto man, and man unto God. (V. 409)

The definition of God and man: Man is an infinite circle whose circumference is nowhere, but the centre is located in one spot; and God is an infinite circle whose circumference is nowhere, but whose centre is everywhere. (II. 33)

The difference between God and the devil is in nothing except in unselfishness and selfishness. The devil knows as much as God, is as powerful as God; only he has no holiness—that makes him a devil. Apply the same idea to the modern world: excess of knowledge and power, without holiness makes human beings devils. (I. 425)

Virtue is that which tends to our improvement, and vice to our degeneration. Man is made up of three qualities—

brutal, human, and godly. That which tends to increase the divinity in you is virtue, and that which tends to increase brutality in you is vice. You must kill the brutal nature and become human, that is loving and charitable. You must transcend that too and become pure bliss, Sachchida-nanda, fire without burning, wonderfully loving, but without the weakness of human love, without the feeling of misery. (VI. 112)

Unsefishness is God. One may live on a throne, in a golden palace, and be perfectly unselfish; and then he is in God. Another may live in a hut and wear rags, and have nothing in the world; yet, if he is selfish, he is intensely merged in the world. (I. 87)

The first sign that you are becoming religious is that you are becoming cheerful. When a man is gloomy, that may be dyspepsia, but it is not religion... Misery is caused by sin, and by no other cause. What business have you with clouded faces? It is terrible. If you have a clouded face, do not go out that day, shut yourself up in your room. What right have you to carry this disease out into the world? (I. 264-65)

Do you not know from the history of the world where the power of the prophets lay? Where was it? In the intellect? Did any of them write a fine book on philosophy, on the most intricate ratiocinations of logic? Not one of them. They only spoke a few words. Feel like Christ and you will be a Christ; feel like Buddha and you will be a Buddha. It is feeling that is the life, the strength, the vitality, without which no amount of intellectual activity can reach God. (II. 307)

In one word, the ideal of *Vedanta* is to know man as he really is, and this is its message, that if you cannot worship your brother man, the manifested God, how can you worship a God who is unmanifested? (II. 325-26)

If you are really pure, how do you see the impure? For what is within,is without. We cannot see impurity without having it inside ourselves. This is one of the practical sides of Vedanta, and I hope that we shall all try to carry it into our lives. (II. 327)

Your godhead is the proof of God Himself. If you are not a prophet there never has been anything true of God. If you are not God, there never was any God, and never will be. This, says the Vedanta, is the ideal to follow. Every one of us will have to become a prophet, and you are that already. Only *know* it. Never think there is anything impossible for the soul. It is the greatest heresy to think so. If there is sin this is the only sin—to say that you are weak, or others are weak. (II. 308)

The *Vedanta* says, there is nothing that is not God... The living God is within you, and yet you are building churches and temples and believing all sorts of imaginary nonsense. The only God to worship is the human soul, in the human body. Of course, all animals are temples too, but man is the highest, the Taj Mahal of temples. If I cannot worship in that, no other temple will be of any advantage. (II. 321)

The secret of religion lies not in theories but in practice. To be good and do good—that is the whole of religion. 'Not he that crieth "Lord", "Lord", but he that doeth the will of the Father.' (VI. 245)

Anything that brings spiritual, mental, or physical weakness, touch it not with the toes of your feet. Religion is the manifestation of the natural strength that is in man. A spring of infinite power is coiled up and is inside this little body, and that spring is spreading itself.... That is the history of man, of religion, civilization, or progress. (VIII. 185)

The basic aim of religion is to bring peace to man. It is not a wise thing for one to suffer in this life so that one can be happy in the next. One must be happy here and now. Any religion that can bring that about is the true religion for humanity. (*Reminiscences of Swami Vivekananda,* p. 45-46)

Whenever any religion succeeds, it must have economic value. Thousands of similar sects will be struggling for power, but only those who meet the real economic problem will have it. Man is guided by the stomach. He walks and the stomach goes first and the head afterwards. Have you not seen that? It will take ages for the head to go first... When children's dreams begin to vanish and you begin to look at things the way they are, the head goes. Just when the head goes first, you go out. (I. 454-55)

Religion deals with the truths of the metaphysical world just as chemistry and the other natural sciences deal with the truths of the physical world. The book one must read to learn chemistry is the book of nature. The book from which to learn religion is your own mind and heart.

The sage is often ignorant of physical science because he reads the wrong book—the book within; and the scientist is too often ignorant of religion because he too reads the wrong book—the book without. (VI.81)

You will find many persons in this world who will say: 'I wanted to become religious, I wanted to realize these things, but have not been able, so I do not believe anything.' Even among the educated you will find these. Large numbers of people will tell you, 'I have tried to be religious all my life, but there is nothing in it'. At the same time, you will find this phenomenon: Suppose man is a chemist, a great scientific man. He comes and tells you this. If you say to him, 'I do not believe anything about chemistry, because I have all my life tried to become a chemist, and do not find anything in it', he will ask, 'When did you try?' When I went to bed, I repeated, "O chemistry, come to me", and it never came.' That is the very same thing. The chemist laughs at you and says: 'Oh, that is not the way. Why did you not go to the laboratory and get all the acids and alkalis and burn your hands from time to time? That alone would have taught you.' Do you take the same trouble with religion? Every science has its own method of learning and religion is to be learned the same way. (VI. 14-15)

Europe, the centre of the manifestation of material energy, will crumble into dust within fifty years, if she is not mindful to change her position, to shift her ground and make spirituality the basis of her life. And what will save Europe is the religion of the *Upanisads*. [Uttered by Swamiji in 1897[(III. 159)

We want to lead mankind to the place where there is neither the Vedas, nor the Bible, nor the Koran; yet this has to be done by harmonizing the Vedas, the Bible, and the Koran. Mankind ought to be taught that religions are but the varied expressions of THE RELIGION, which is Oneness, so that each may choose the path that suits him best. (VI. 416)

Be moral. Be brave. Be a heart-whole man—strictly moral brave unto desperation. Don't bother your head with religious theories. Cowards only sin, brave men never, no, not even in mind. (V. 1)

The only definition that can be given of mortality is this: *That which is selfish is immoral, and that which is unselfish is moral*. (I. 110)

One man may speak beautiful language and beautiful thought, but they do not impress people; another man speaks neither beautiful language nor beautiful thoughts, yet his words charm. Every movement of his is powerful. That is the power of *Ojas*....It is only the chaste man or woman who can make the *Ojas* rise and store it in the brain; that is why chastity has always been considered the highest virtue. A man feels that if he is unchaste, spirituality goes away, he loses mental vigour and moral stamina. That is why in all the religious orders in the world, which have produced spiritual giants, you will always find absolute chastity insisted upon. (I. 169-70)

Ethics always say, 'Not I, but thou.' Its motto is: 'Not self, but non-self.' The vain ideas of individualism, to which man clings when he is trying to find that infinite Power or that infinite Pleasure through the senses, have to be given up—say the laws of ethics. You have to put *yourself* last, and others before you. The senses say, 'Myself first.' Ethics says, 'I must hold myself last'. Thus, all codes of ethics are based upon this renunciation; destruction, not construction, of the individual on the material plane. That Infinite will never find expression upon the material plane, nor is it possible or thinkable. (II. 62-63)

Utilitarian standards cannot explain the ethical relations of men, for, in the first place, we cannot derive any ethical laws from considerations of utility. The utilitarian wants us to give up the struggle after the Infinite, the reaching-out for the Supersensuous, as impracticable and absurd, and in the same breath, asks us to take up ethics and do good to society. Why should we do good? Doing good is a secondary consideration. We must have an ideal. Ethics itself is not the end, but the means to the end. If the end is not there, why should we be ethical? Why should I do good to other men, and and not injure them? If happiness is the goal of mankind, why should I not make myself happy and others unhappy? What prevents me? In the second place, the basis of utility is too narrow... Utilitarian theories can only work under present social conditions. Beyond that they have no value. But a morality, an ethical code, derived from religion and spirituality, has the whole of infinite man for its scope. It takes up the individual, but its relations are to the Infinite, and it takes up society also—because society is nothing but numbers of these individuals grouped together.(II. 63-64)

(VI) Man The Maker of His Destiny

What do I care if Mohammed was a good-man, or Buddha! Does that alter *my* own goodness or evil? Let us be good for our own sake on our own responsibility! Not because somebody way back there was good! (*Reminiscences of Swami Vivekananda*, p. 273)

We are responsible for what we are, and whatever we wish ourselves to be, we have the power to make ourselves. If what we are now has been the result of our own past actions, it certainly follows that whatever we wish to be in future can be produced by our present actions; so we have to know how to act. (I. 31)

This human body is the greatest body in the universe, and a human being the greatest being. Man is higher than all animals, than all angels; none is greater than man. (I. 142)

Man is man, so long as he is struggling to rise above nature, and this nature is both internal and external... And if we read the history of nations between the lines, we shall always find that the rise of a nation comes with an increase in the number of such men; and the fall begins when this pursuit after the Infinite, however vain the Utilitarians may call it, has ceased. That is to say, the mainspring of the strength of every race lies in its spirituality, and the death of that race begins the day that spirituality wanes and materialism gains ground. (II. 64-65)

This world is the great gymnasium where we come to make ourselves strong. (V. 410)

All healthy social changes are the mainfestations of the spiritual forces working within, and if these are strong and well adjusted, society will arrange itself accordingly. Each individual has to work out his own salvation; there is no other way, and so also with nations. ...It is very easy to point out the defects of institutions, all being more or less imperfect, but he is the real benefactor of humanity who helps the individual to overcome his imperfections under whatever institutions he may live. The individuals being raised, the nation and its instructions are bound to rise. (V. 415-16)

You have to grow from inside out. None can teach you, none can make you spiritual. There is no other teacher but your own soul. (V. 410)

Men in general lay all the blame of life on their fellowmen, or, failing that, on God, or they conjure up a ghost, and say it is fate. Where is fate, and who is fate? We reap what we sow. We are the makers of our own fate. None else has the blame, none has the praise. The wind is blowing; those vessels whose sails are unfurled catch it, and go forward on their way, but those which have their sails furled do not catch the wind. Is that the fault of the wind? (II. 224)

Say, 'This misery that I am suffering is of my own doing, and that very thing proves that it will have to be undone by me alone.' That which I created, I can demolish; that which is created by someone else, I shall never be able to destroy. Therefore, stand up, be bold, be strong. Take the whole responsibility on your own shoulders, and know that you are the creator of your own destiny. All the strength and succour you want is within yourselves. (II. 225)

Make your own future. 'Let the dead past bury its dead.' The infinite future is before you, and you must always remember that each word, thought, and deed lays up a store for you, and that as the bad thoughts and bad works are ready to spring up like tigers, so also there is the inspiring hope that the good thoughts and good deeds are ready with the power of a hundred thousand angels to defend you always and for ever. (II. 225)

'Ours not to reason why, ours but to do and die.' Be of good cheer and believe that we are selected by the Lord to do great things, and we will do them. (V. 23)

Unfortunately, in this life, the cast majority of persons are groping through this dark life without any ideal at all. If a man with an ideal makes a thousand mistakes, I am sure that the man without an ideal makes fifty thousand. Therefore, it is better to have an ideal. (II. 152)

Man begins to struggle and fight against nature. He makes many mistakes, he suffers. But eventually, he conquers nature and realizes his freedom. When he is free, nature becomes his slave.(VIII. 249)

I disagree with the idea that freedom is obedience to the laws of nature, I do not understand what that means. According to the history of human progress, it is disobedience to nature that has constituted that progress. (VIII. 257)

For the world can be good and pure, only if our lives are good and pure. It is an effect, and we are the means. Therefore, let us purify ourselves. Let us make ourselves perfect. (II. 9)

What is the use of fighting and complaining? That will not help us to better things. He who grumbles at the little thing that has fallen to his lot to do, will grumble at everything. Always grumbling, he will lead a miserable life, and everything will be a failure. But that man who does his duty as he goes, putting his shoulder to the wheel, will see the light, and higher and higher duties will fall to his share. (V. 242)

Do not fly away from the wheels of the world-machine, but stand inside it and learn the secret of work. Though proper work done inside, it is also possible to come out. (I. 115)

Every thought that we think, every deed that we do, after a certain time becomes fine, goes into seed form, so to speak, and lives in the fine body in a potential form, and after a time it emerges again and bears its results. These results condition the life of man. Thus he moulds his own life. Man is not bound by any other laws excepting those which he makes for himself. (II. 348)

My ideal, indeed, can be put into a few words, and that is: to preach unto mankind their divinity, and how to make it manifest in every movement of life. (VII. 498)

Purity, patience, and perseverance are the three essentials to success, and above all—love. (VI. 281)

Life is ever expanding, contraction is death. The self-seeking man who is looking after his personal comforts and leading a lazy life—there is no room for him even in hell. (VI. 294)

I am sure God will pardon a man who will use his reason and cannot believe, rather than a man who believes blindly instead of using the faculties He has given him... We must reason; and when reason proves to us the truth of these prophets and great men about whom the ancient books speak in every country, we shall believe in them. We shall believe in them when we see such prophets among ourselves. We shall then find that they were not peculiar men, but only illustrations of certain principles. (VI. 12-13)

Why should you not try to hit the mark? We become wiser through failures. Time is infinite. Look at the wall. Did the wall ever tell a lie? It is always the wall. Man tells a lie-and becomes a good, to. It is better to do something; never mind even if it proves to be wrong; it is better than doing nothing. The cow never tells a lie; but she remains a cow, all the time. Do something! (IV. 126-27)

Go on doing good, thinking holy thoughts continuously, that is the only way to suppress base impressions. Never say any man is hopeless, because he only represents a character, a bundle of ha bits, which can be checked by new and better ones. Character is repeated habits, and repeated habits alone can reform character... The chaste brain has tremendous energy and gigantic will power. (I. 208, 263)

We can overcome the difficulty by constant practice. We must learn that nothing can happen to us, unless we make ourselves susceptible. (II. 7)

I was once travelling in the Himalayas and the long road stretched before us. We poor monks cannot get anyone to carry us, so we had to make all the way on foot. There was an old man with us... He said, 'Oh, Sir, how to cross it; I cannot walk any more; my chest will break.' I said to him, 'Look down at your feet.' He did so, and I said, 'The road that is under your feet is the road that you have passed over and is the same road that you see before you; it will soon be under your feet.' The highest things are under your feet, because you are Divine Stars. (VIII. 186-87)

'It is the coward and the fool who says, "That is fate'- so says the Sanskrit proverb. But it is the strong man who stands up and says, 'I will make my fate.' It is people who are getting old who talk of fate. Young men generally do not come to astrology. (VIII. 184)

You really want to judge the character of a man, look not at his great performances. Every fool may become a hero at one time or another. Watch a man do his most common action; those are indeed the things which will tell you the real character of a great man. Great occasions rouse even the lowest of human beings to some kind of greatness, but he alone is the really great man whose character is great, always, the same wherever he be. (I. 29)

Every good thought that we send to the world, without thinking of any return, will be stored up there and break one link in the chain, and make us purer and purer, until we become the purest of mortals. (I. 116)

If you project hatred and jealousy, they will rebound on you with compound interest. No power can avert them; when once you have put them in motion, you will have to bear them. Remembering this will prevent you from doing wicked things. (I. 262)

Everything is conscious which rebels against nature: there, conscious is manifested. Just try to kill a little ant, even it will once resist to save its life. Where there is struggle, where there is rebellion, there is the sign of life, there consciousness is manifested. (VI. 453)

Isn't it man that makes money? Where did you ever hear of money making man? If you can, I say, make yourself one in speech and action, money will pour in at your feet of itself, like. (VI. 455)

The road to the Good is the roughest and steppes in the universe. It is a wonder that so many succeed, no wonder that so many fall. Character has to be established through a thousand stumbles. (VIII. 383)

Each work has to pass through these stages—ridicule, opposition, and then acceptance. Each man who thinks ahead of his time is sure to be misunderstood. So opposition and persecution are welcome ,only I have to be steady and pure and must have immense faith in God, and all these will vanish. (V. 91)

Each soul is potentially divine. The goal is to manifest this divinity within by controlling nature, external and internal. Do this either by work, or worship, or psychic control, or philosophy—by one, or more, or all of these—and be free. This is the whole of religion. Doctrines, or dogmas, or rituals, or books, or temples, or forms, are but secondary details. (I. 257)

Each one thinks his method is best. Very good! But remember, it may be good for you. One food which is very indigestible to one is very digestible to another. Because it is good for you, do not jump to the conclusion that your method is everybody's method, that Jack's coat fits John and Mary. All the uneducated, uncultured, unthinking men and women have been put into that sort of strait jacket! Think for yourselves. Become atheists! Become materialists! That would be better. Exercise the mind! What right have you to say that this man's method is wrong? It may be wrong for you. That is to say, if you undertake the method, you will be degraded; but that does not mean that he will be degraded. Therefore, if you have knowledge and see a man weak, do not condemn him. Go to his level and help him if you can. He must grow. I can put five bucket-fuls of knowledge into his head in five hours. But what good will it do? He will be a little worse than before. (I. 470)

Go and preach to all: 'Arise, awake, sleep no more; within each of you, there is the power to remove all wants and all miseries. Believe this, and that power will be manifested.'.. If you can think that infinite power, infinite knowledge, and indomitable energy lies within you, and if you can bring out that power, you also can become like me. (VI. 454)

(VII) India: Our Motherland

Shall India die? Then from the world all spirituality will be extinct, all moral perfection will be extinct, all sweet-souled sympathy for religion will be extinct, all ideality will be extinct; and in its place will reign the duality of lust and luxury as the male and female deities, with money as its priest; fraud, force, and competition its ceremonies; and the human soul its sacrifice. Such a thing can never be... Will she die? This old Mother of all that is noble or moral or spiritual, the land which the sages trod, the land in which Godlike men still live and breathe? I will borrow the lantern of the Athenian sage and follow you, my brother, through the cities and villages, plains and forests, of this broad world—show me such men in other lands if you can. (IV.347-48)

The debt which the world owes to our Motherland is immense. Taking country with country, there is not one race on this earth to which the world owes so much as to the patient Hindu, the mild Hindu... Here activity prevailed when even Greece did not exist, when Rome was not thought of, when the very fathers of the modern Europeans lived in the forests and painted themselves blue. Even earlier, when history has no record, and tradition dares not peer into the gloom of that intense past, even from then until now, but every word has been spoken with a blessing behind it, and peace before it. (III. 105-06)

Can you adduce any reason why India should lie in the ass-tide of the Aryan nations? Is she inferior in intellect? Is she inferior in dexterity? Can you look art, her mathematics, at her philosophy, and answer 'yes? All that is needed is that she should de-hypnotize herself and wake up from her age-long sleep to take her true rank in the hierarchy of nations... The national ideals of India are Renunciation and Service. Intensify her in those channels, 'and the rest will take care of itself. (V. 227-28)

This national ship of ours, ye children of the Immortals, my countrymen, has been plying for ages carrying civilization and enriching the whole world with its inestimable treasure. For scores of shining centuries, this national ship of ours has been ferrying across the ocean of life, and has taken millions of souls to the other shore, beyond all misery. But today, it may have sprung a leak and got damaged, through your own fault or whatever cause, it matters not. What would you, who have placed yourselves in it, do now? Would you go about cursing it and quarrelling among yourselves! Would you not all unite together and put your best efforts to stop the holes? Let us all gladly give our hearts' blood to do it; and if we fail in the attempt, let us all sink and die together, with blessings and not curses on our lips. (III. 461)

Now you understand clearly where the soul of this ogress is: it is in religion. Because no one was able to destroy that, therefore the Hindu nation is still living, having survived so many troubles and tribulations. Well, one Indian scholar asks, 'What is the use of keeping the soul of the nation in religion? Why not keep it in social or political independence, as is the case with other nations? It is very ways to talk like that. . . The fact is: that the river has come down a thousand miles from its source in the mountains; does it, or can it, go back to its source? If it ever tries to trace back its course, it will simply dry up by being dissipated in all directions. Anyhow, the river is sure to fall into the ocean, sooner or later, either by passing through open and beautiful plains or struggling through grimy soil. If our national life of these ten thousand years has been a mistake, then there is no help for it; and if we try now to form a new character, the inevitable result will be that we shall die. (V. 459-60)

Hidden under the ashes of apparent death, the fire of our national life is yet smouldering and the life of this nation is religion, its language religion, and its idea religion; and your politics, society, municipality, plague prevention work, and famine relief work—all these things will be done as they have been done all along here, viz. only through religion; otherwise all your frantic yelling and bewailing will end in nothing, my friend! (V. 461)

In every country, the means is the same after all, that is whatever only a handful of powerful men dictate, becomes the *fait accompli*; the rest of the men only follow like a flock of sheep, that's all. I have seen your Parliament, your Senate, your vote, majority, ballot; it is the same thing everywhere, my friend . . . Now the question is this, who are these men of power in India—they who are giants in religion. It is they who lead our society; and it is they again who change our social laws and usages when necessity demands; and we listen to them silently and do what they command. (V. 461)

First of all, try to understand this: Does man make laws, or do laws make man? Does man make money, or does money make man? Does man make name and dame, or name and fame make man? Be a man first, my friend, and you will see how all those things and the rest will follow of themselves after you. Give up that hateful malice, that dog-like bickering and barking at one another, and take your stand on good purpose, right means, righteous courage, and be brave. When you are born a man, leave some indelible mark behind you. (V. 462)

None will be able to resist truth and love and sincerity. Are you sincere? Unselfish even unto death? And loving? Then fear not, not even death. Onward, my lads! The whole world requires Light. It is expectant! India alone has that Light, not in magic mummeries, and chariatanism, but in the teaching of the glories of the spirit of real religion-of the highest spiritual truth. That is why the Lord has preserved the race through all its vicissitudes unto the present day. Now the time has come. Have faith that you are all, my brave lads, born to do great things! Let not the barks of puppies frighten you—no, not even the thunderbolts of heaven—but stand up and work. (V. 43)

India will be raised, not with the power of the flesh, but with the power of the spirit; not with the flag for destruction, but with the flag of peace and love. One vision I see clear as life before me, that the ancient Mother has awakened once more, sitting on Her throne—rejuvenated, more glorious than ever. Proclaim Her to all the world with the voice of peace and benediction. (IV. 352-53)

Let New India arise—out of the peasants' cottage, grasping the plough; out of the huts of the fisherman, the cobbler and the sweeper. Let her spring from the grocer's shop, from beside the oven of the fritter-seller. Let her emanate from the factory, from marts and from markets. Let her emerge from groves and forests, from hills and mountains. (VII. 327)

We Indians suffer from a great defect, viz. we cannot make a permanent organization—and the reason is that we never like to share power with others and never think of what will come after we are gone. (VIII. 456-57)

An English friend of mine, named General Strong, was in India during the Sepoy Mutiny. He used to tell many stories about it. One day, in the course of conversation, I asked him how it was that the sepoys who had enough of guns, ammunition, and provisions at their disposal, and were also trained veterans, came to suffer such a defeat. He replied that the leaders among them, instead of advancing forward, only kept shouting from a sate position in the rear, 'Fight on, brave lads', and so forth; but unless the commanding officer goes ahead and faces death, the rank and file will never fight with heart. 'A captain must sacrifice his head.' If you can lay down your life for a cause, then only you can be a leader. But we all want to be leaders without making the necessary sacrifice. And the result is zero—nobody listens to us! (VII. 325-26)

Learn obedience first. Among these western nations, with such a high spirit of independence; the spirit of obedience is equally strong. We are all of us self-important, which never produces any work. Great enterprise, boundless courage, tremendous energy, and above all, perfect obedience—these are the only traits that lead to individual and national regeneration. These traits are altogether lacking in us. (VI. 349)

Jealousy is the bane of our national character, natural to slaves. Even the Lord worth all His power could do nothing on account of this jealousy. Think of me as one who has done all his duty and is now dead and gone. Think that the whole work is upon your shoulders. Think that you, younger men of our motherland, are destined to do this. Put yourselves to the task. (IV. 359-60)

I am thoroughly convinced that no individual or nation can live by holding itself apart from the community of others. Give and take is the law' and if India wants to raise herself once more, it is absolutely necessary that she brings out her treasures and throws them broadcast among the nations of the earth, and in return be ready to receive what others have to give her. Expansion is life, contraction is death. Love is life, and hatred is death. We commenced to die the day we began to hate other races; and nothing can prevent our death unless we come back to expansion, which is life. (IV. 365-66)

I consider that the great national sin is the neglect of the masses, and that is one of the causes of our downfall. No amount of politics would be of any avail, until the masses in India are once more well educated, well fed, and well cared for. They pay for our education, they build our temples, but in return they get kicks. They are practically our slaves. If we want to regenerate India, we must work for them. (V. 222-23)

The more, therefore, the Hindus study the past, the more glorious will be their future, and whoever tries to bring the past to the door of everyone, is a great benefactor to his nation. The degeneration of India came not because the laws and customs of the ancients were bad, but because they were not allowed to be carried to their legitimate conclusions. (IV. 324)

There are many things to be done, but means are wanting in this country. We have brains, but no hands. We have the doctrine of Vedanta, but we have not the power to reduce it into practice. In our books there is the doctrine of universal equality, but in work we make great distinctions. It was in India that unselfish and disinterested work of the most exalted type was preached, but in practice we are awfully cruel, awfully heartless—unable to think of anything besides our own mass-of-flesh bodies . . . I too believe that India will awake again, if anyone could love with all his heart the people of the country—bereft of the grace of affluence, of blasted fortune, their discretion totally lost, down-trodden, ever-starved, quarrelsome, and envious. Then only will India awake, when hundreds of large-hearted men and women, giving up all desires of enjoying the luxuries of life, will long and exert themselves to their utmost for the wellbeing of the millions of their countrymen who are gradually sinking lower and lower in the vortex of destitution and ignorance. (V. 125-26)

The one thing that is at the root of all evils in India is the condition of the poor. The poor in the West are devils; compared to them, ours are angels, and it is therefore so much the easier to raise our poor. The only service to be done for our lower classes is to give them education, *to develop their lost individuality*. (IV. 363)

For the last three-quarters of a century, India has been bubbling over with reform societies and reformers. But, alas, every one of them has proved a failure. They did not know the secret. They had not learned the great lesson to be learned.

In their haste, they laid all the evils in our society at the door of religion; and, like the man in the story, wanting to kill the mosquito that sat on a friend's forehead, they were trying to deal such heavy blows as would have killed man and mosquito together. But in this case, fortunately, they only dashed themselves against immovable rocks, and were crushed out of existence in the shock of recoil. Glory unto those noble and unselfish souls who have struggled and failed in their misdirected attempts. Those galvanic shocks of reformatory zeal were necessary to rouse the sleeping leviathan. But they were entirely destructive, and not constructive, and as such, they were mortal, and therefore died. Let us bless them and profit by their experience. Until all the Hindu race becomes extinct, and a new race takes possession the of land, such a thing never be European until she dies. (IV. 347)

But mark you, if you give up that spirituality, leaving it aside to go after the materializing civilization of the West, the result will be that in three generations you will be an extinct race; because the backbone of the nation will be broken, the foundation upon which the national edifice has been built will be undermined, and the result will be annihilation all round. (III. 153)

Let us all work hard, my brethren; this is no time for sleep. On our work depends the coming of the India of the future. She is there ready waiting. She is only sleeping. Arise and awake, and see her seated here, on her eternal throne, rejuvenated, more glorious than she ever was—this motherland of ours. (III. 154)

Utter no words of condemnation. Close your lips, and let your hearts open. Work out the salvation of this land and of the whole world, each of you thinking that the entire burden is on your shoulders. Carry the light and the life of the Vedanta to every door, and rouse up the divinity that is hidden within every soul. (III. 199)

Make your nerves strong. What we want is muscles of iron and nerves of steel. We have wept long enough. No more weeping, but stand on your feet and be men. (III. 224)

Be steady, and above all, be pure and sincere to the backbone. Have faith in your destiny... It depends upon you who have no money; because you are poor, therefore you will work. Because you have nothing, therefore you will be sincere. Because you are sincere, you will be ready to renounce all. That is what I am just now telling you. (III. 445)

Feel, my children, feel; feel for the poor, the ignorant, the down trodden; feel till the heart stops and the brain reels and you think you will go mad; then pour the soul out at the feet of the Lord, and then will come power, help, and indomitable energy. Struggle, struggle, was my motto for the last ten years. Struggle, still sat I. When it was all dark, I used to say, struggle; when light is breaking in, I still say, struggle. Be not afraid, my children. (IV. 367)

Have fire and spread all over. Work work. Be the servant while leading. Be unselfish, and *never listen to one friend in private accusing another*. Have infinite patience, and success is yours. ... Take care! Beware of everything that is untrue: stick to truth, and we shall succeed, maybe slowly, but surely. Work as if on each of you depended the whole work. Fifty centuries are looking on you, the future of India depends on you. Work on. (IV. 369-70)

My faith is in the younger generation, the modern generation, out of them will come my workers. They will work out the whole problem, like lions. I have formulated the idea and have given my life to it. They will spread from centre to centre, until we have covered the whole of India. (V. 223)

What we want are some young men who will renounce everything and sacrifice their lives for their country's sake. We should first form their lives and then some real work can be expected. (V. 352)

Even the least work done for others awakens the power within; even thinking the least good of others gradually instils into the heart the strength of a lion. I love you all ever so much, but I wish you all to die working for others—I should rather be glad to see you do that ! . . . Get up, and put your shoulders to the wheel—how long is this life for? As you have come into this world, leave some mark behind. Otherwise, where is the difference between you and the trees and strones? (V. 382-83)

We now mostly need the idea of a hero with the tremendous spirit of *rajas* thrilling through his veins from head to foot—the hero who will dare and die to know the Truth—the hero whose armour is renunciation, whose sword is wisdom. We want now the spirit of the brave warrior in the battlefield of life, and not of the wooing lover who looks upon life as a pleasure-garden! (V. 388)

Have faith in yourself. You people were once the Vedic *rsis*. Only, you have come in different forms, that's all. I see it clear as daylight that you all have infinite power in you. Rouse that up; arise, arise-apply yourselves heart and soul, gird up your loins. What will you do with wealth and fame that are so transitory? Do you know what I think -I don't care for *mukti* and all that. My mission is to arouse within you all such ideas; rebirth to train up a single man. (VII. 176)

My boy, when death is inevitable, is it not better to die like heroes than as stocks and stones? And what is the use of living a day or two more in this transitory world? It is better to wear out than to rust out-specially for the sake of doing the least good to others. (VII. 176)

Within no strength in body, no enthusiasm at heart, and no originality in the brain, what will they do-these lumps of dead matter! By stimulating them, I want to bring life into them—to this, I have dedicated my life. I will rouse them through the infallible power of Vedic *mantras*. I am born to proclaim to them that fearless message—'Arise, Awake!" Be you my helpers in this work. (VIII. 182)

Numbers do not count, nor does wealth or poverty; a handful of men can throw the world off its hinges, provided they are united in thought, word and deed—never forget this conviction. The more opposition there is, the better. The more opposition there is, the better. Does a river acquire velocity unless there is resistance? The newer and better a thing is, the more opposition which foretells success. (VIII. 372)

But appreciation or no appreciation, I am born to organize these young men; nay, hundreds more in every city are ready to join me; and I want to send them rolling like irresistible waves over India, bringing comfort, morality, religion, education to the doors of the meanest and the most downtrodden. And this, I will do or die. (VIII. 298)

If you are really my children, you will fear nothing, stop at nothing. You will be like lions. We must rouse India and the whole world . . . My children must be ready to jump into fire, if needed, to accomplish their work. (V. 61-62)

O India! Forget not that the ideal of thy womanhood is Sita, Savitri, Damayanti; forget not that the God thou worshippest is the great Ascetic of ascetics, the all-renouncing Sankara, the Lord of Uma; forget not that thy marriage, thy wealth, thy life are not for sense-pleasure, are not for thy individual personal happiness; forget not that thou art born as a sacrifice to the Mother's altar . . . forget not that the lower classes, the ignorant, the poor, the illiterate, the cobbler, the sweeper, are thy flesh and blood, thy brothers. (IV. 479-80)

Go, all of you, wherever there is an outbreak of plague or famine, or wherever the people are in distress, and mitigate their suffering.

At the most, you may die in the attempt, what of that? How many like you are being born and dying like worms every day? What difference does that make to the world at large? Die you must, but have a great ideal to die for, and it is better to die with a great ideal in life. (V. 383-84)

You must not depend on any *foreign help*. Nations, like individuals, must help themselves. This is real patriotism. If a nation cannot do that, its time has not yet come. It must wait. (V. 108)

Work unto death—I am with you, and when I am gone, my spirit will work with you. This life comes and goes—wealth, fame, enjoyments are only of a few days. It is better, afar better to die on the field of duty, preaching the truth, than to die like a worldly worm. Advance! (V. 114)

(VIII) Other Exhortations

Be not anxious. It is against the big tree that the great wind strikes. 'Poking a fire makes it burn better'; 'A snake struck on the head raised its hood' - and so on. When there comes affliction in the heart, when the storm of sorrow blows all around, and it seems light will be seen no more, when hope and courage are almost gone, it is then, in the midst of this great spiritual tempest, that the light of Brahman within gleams. Brought up in the lap of luxury, lying on a bed of roses, and never shedding a tear, who has ever become great, who has ever unfolded the Brahman within? (IV. 492)

When there is conflict between the heart and the brain, let the heart be followed, because intellect has only one state, reason and within that, intellect works, and cannot get beyond. It is the heart which takes one to the highest plane, which intellect can never reach; it goes beyond intellect, and reaches to what is called inspiration . . . Men of heart get the butter and the 'buttermilk' is left for the intellectual. (I. 412-13)

Let us all be honest. If we cannot follow the ideal, let us confess our weakness, but not degrade it, let not any try to pull it down. (IV. 145)

You must remember that humanity travels not from error to truth, but from truth to truth; it may be, if you like it better, from lower truth to higher truth, but never from error to truth. (IV. 147)

The lower the organization, the greater the pleasure in the senses. Very few man can eat a meal with the same gusto as a dog or a wolf. But all the pleasures of the dog or the wolf have gone, as it were, into the senses. The lower types of humanity in all nations find pleasure in the senses, while the cultured and the educated find it in sciences. Spirituality is a still higher plane. (II. 66)

The history of the world is the history of persons like Buddha and Jesus. The passionless and unattached do most for the world. (VIII. 226)

Every successful man must have behind him somewhere tremendous integrity, tremendous sincerity, and that is the cause of his signal success in life. He may not have been perfectly unselfish; yet he was tending towards it. If he had been perfectly unselfish, his would have been as great a success as that of the Buddha or of the Christ. The degree of unselfishness marks the degree of success everywhere. (V. 240)

Truth, purity, and unselfishness—wherever these are present, there is no power below or above the sun to crush the possessor thereof. Equipped with these, one individual is able to face the whole universe in opposition. (IV. 279)

Go on! Do not look back if you think you have done something that is not right. Now, do you believe you could be what you are today, had you not made those mistakes before? Bless your mistakes, then. They have been angels unawares. Blessed be torture! Blessed be happiness! Do not care what be your lot. Hold on to the ideal. March on! (V. 253)

Doing good to others is a virtue (*dharma*), injuring others is sin. Strength and manliness are virtue; weakness and cowardice are sin. Independence is virtue; dependence is sin. Loving others is virtue; hating others is sin. Faith in God and in one's own Self is virtue; doubt is sin. Knowledge of oneness is virtue; seeing diversity is sin. (V. 419)

In modern times, if a man quotes a Moses, or a Buddha, or a Christ, he is laughed at; but let him give the name of a Huxely, a Tyndall, or a Dareain, and it is swallowed without salt. 'Huxley has said it', that is enough for many. We are free from superstitions, indeed! That was a religious superstition, and this is a scientific superstition, only, in and through that superstition came life-giving ideas of spirituality; in and through this modern superstition come lust and greed. That superstition was worship of God, and this superstition is worship of filthy lucre, of fame, of power. That is the difference. (II. 74)

True equality has never been and never can be on earth. How can we all be equal here? This impossible kind of equality implies total death. What makes the difference between man and man? It is largely the difference in the brain. Nowadays, no one but a lunatic will say that we are all born with the same brain power. (I. 113-14)

My whole ambition in life is to set in motion a machinery which will bring noble ideas to the door of everybody, and then let men and women settle their own fate. Let them know what our forefathers as well as other nations have thought on the most momentous questions of life. Let them see specially what others are doing new, and then decide. We are to put the chemicals together, the crystallization will be done by nature according to her laws. Work hard, be steady. Keep the motto before you: Elevation of the masses without injuring their religion. (V. 29)

Let people praise you or blame you, let fortune smile or frown upon you, let your body fall today or after a *yuga*, see that you do not deviate from the path of Truth. How much of tempests and waves one had to weather, before one reaches the haven of Peace. The greater a man has become, the fiercer ordeal he has had to pass through. (VII. 126)

It is my firm conviction that no great work is accomplished in this world by low cunning. (VII. 125)

This I have seen in life—he who is overcautious about himself falls into dangers at every step; he who is afraid of losing honour and respect, gets only disgrace; he who is always afraid of loss always loses. (VIII. 433)

I know my mission in life, and no chauvinism about me; I belong as much to India as to the world. ..Do you mean to say I am born to live and die one of those caste-ridden, superstitions, merciless, hypocritical, atheistic *cowards* that you find only amongst the educated Hindus? I hate cowardice; I will have nothing to do with cowards or political nonsense. I do not believe in any politics. God and truth, else is trash. (V. 95-96)

If I do not find bliss in the life of the Spirit, shall I seek satisfaction in the life of the senses? If I cannot get nectar, shall I fall back upon ditch water? (V. 417)

10

Places In India Closely Associated with Vivekananda

Although the whole world was Vivekananda's avenue, yet there are a few places is India which are closely associated with his name. A brief description of those places is given below:

(I) *Almora*: This all-weather hill resort in the Kumaon Hills of Uttaranchal is famous for its salubrious climate, natural beauty and snow-capped mountain peaks. Perhaps it was its peaceful and natural pulchritude which attracted the Swani's attention. In 1899 he had established the Advait Ahshram at Mayawati, a place near the town which had been quite a centre for publishing various magazines started at Vivekananda's inspiration.

(II) *Belur Math*: Situated on the west bank of the Ganga, five miles above Calcutta, it is now the headquarters of the international Ramakrishan Mission. This mission was founded by Vivekananda in 1887, immediately after the death of his mentor and Master. The Belur Math (monastery), a modern shrine with a temple, a mosque and a church seen from different directions, convey the message of Swami

Vivekananda that it is only due to different points of view that all faith appear different but essentially they all teach one precept. Twenty month of the city of Calcutta and across the river Hooghly, just opposite Belur Math stands the famous Kali Temple of Dakshineshwar. Associated with Rama Krishna Paramhanse and also with Vivekananda, its main shrine houses the image of Goddess Kali the chosen deity of the Paramahanse standing on the prostrate Shiv.

(III) *Vivekananda Rock Memorial (Kanya Kumari):* Kanyakumari is India's Land's End, the tip of peninsular India where the Bay of Bengal, the India ocean and the Arabian Sea meet. Close to the temple dedicated to Kanyakumari, one of the incarnations of Parvati Goddess, off shore stand two huge rocks where Vivekananda had once meditated. One of them had now the Vivekananda Rock Memorial with Swami's statute on it. The swami had daringly seen across this, 'sharp infested creek' only for reaching this rock and having mental view of whole of India with a detached perception. The statue was built in 1970. Trivandrum (Kerala) is the nearest (87 kms.) rail head. Buses are also available from Madras. Now this place has emerged into a cool and calm tourist centre. There is also an establishment of the R.K. Mission.